WOOD DECKS:

CONSTRUCTION & MAINTENANCE

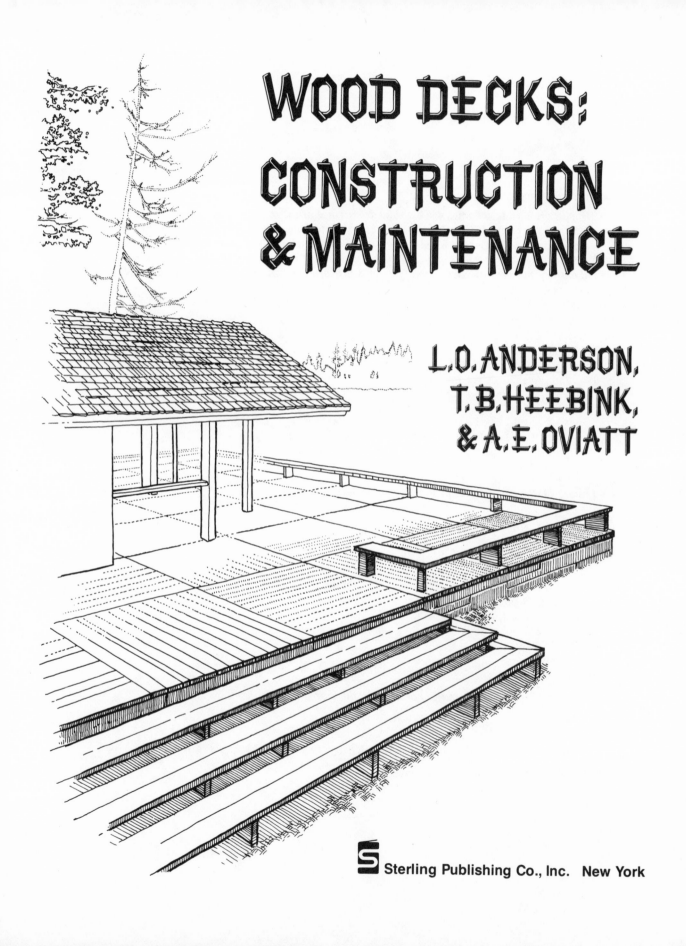

WOOD DECKS: CONSTRUCTION & MAINTENANCE

L.O. ANDERSON,
T.B. HEEBINK,
& A.E. OVIATT

Sterling Publishing Co., Inc. New York

Acknowledgment

*The authors wish to acknowledge the valued assistance of the organizations listed on page 5
of the report. Particular thanks are expressed to the technical staffs of the American Plywood
Association and the Western Wood Products Association who helped develop Tables 2 through 6
and who reviewed the report in draft stage. Also, to staff members of the U.S. Forest Products
Laboratory and the American Wood Preservers Institute for their helpful reviews of the draft.*

Published in 1980 by
Sterling Publishing Co., Inc.
Two Park Avenue
New York, N.Y. 10016

Library of Congress Cataloging in Publication Data

Anderson, LeRoy Oscar, 1905-
　　Wood decks.

　　Bibliography: p.
　　1. Decks (Architecture, Domestic). 2. Building,
Wooden. I. Heebink, Thomas Bruce, 1914-　　joint
author. II. Oviatt, A. E., joint author. III. Title.
TH4970.A53　　　690'.1'8　　　77-6961
ISBN 0-8069-8974-4
Previously
ISBN 0-8473-1569-x

Photographs provided by courtesy of Casey & the Carpenter, Brooklyn, N. Y.

Originally published in 1972 under the title *Construction Guides for Exposed Wood Decks.*

Printed in the United States of America

Figure 1. — Sheltered decks extend living areas.

CONTENTS

Introduction

Outdoor living is becoming a way of life for the American family. Moderate seasons and climates stimulate special enthusiasm for outdoor living. Thus, there is a desire for the outdoor "living room," an area adjacent to the home for family enjoyment in pleasant weather.

This outdoor living area is often provided by a wood deck that adds spaciousness to a home at modest cost. A deck can expand or frame a view to increase a homeowner's enjoyment. It can serve as an adult entertainment center by night and a children's play area by day — being easily adapted to the activity or degree of formality desired.

Decks, which may offer the only means of providing outdoor living areas for steep hillside homes, have gained popularity for homes on level ground — as a way of adding charm, style, and livability. To achieve these gains, wood decks offer a variety of flexible, economical systems, and this publication suggests ways to insure the greatest satisfaction from such systems.

Types of Decks

Most of the decks considered here are low- or high-level decks with spaced floor boards and are attached to the house for access and partial support. There are, in addition, detached low-level decks and rooftop decks. The latter are simpler than others in some respects since they rely on the roof for primary support but do introduce a need to prevent leakage to the space below. Solid decks may be made of caulked planking or of plywood with a waterproof coating such as an elastomeric wearing surface.

Low-level wood decks may be chosen for their non-reflective and resilient qualities in preference to a paved patio . More frequently, the wood deck is chosen because of its design versatility and adaptability to varied use.

Low-level decks can be simply supported on concrete piers or short posts closely spaced, thereby simplifying the main horizontal structure. However, drainage can be a problem on low or level ground and provision to insure good drainage should be made before the deck is built. Good drainage not only keeps the ground firm to adequately support the deck but avoids dampness that could encourage decay in posts or sills.

Hillside decks were first in the line of residential decks — used as a means of creating outdoor living areas on steep sites. Despite their expense as compared with a level yard or patio, they add living area at much less cost than that of indoor space. Moreover, the outdoor setting adds a new dimension to the home and provides amenities that people prize.

The substructure of hillside decks is designed to provide solid support with a minimum number of members, especially if exposed to view from below. This may require a heavier deck structure and more substantial railings than are needed for low-level decks, but the general rules to insure satisfactory performance are the same.

Rooftop decks may cover a carport roof or a room of the house. One constructed over a carport may be relatively simple to build but may be difficult to handle aesthetically.

Where a rooftop provides the deck support, it may also serve as the floor, particularly if the deck is included in the initial construction. The roof must then be designed as a floor to support

Figure 2. — Low-level decks may feature simple construction.

Figure 3. — High-level decks can improve privacy and outlook.

the deck loads. If the deck is added to a completed house, it is more common to construct a separate deck floor over the roof.

Planning a Deck

A first step in planning a deck is to determine the requirements and limitations of the local building code. Limitations on height and width and required floor loads or railing resistance vary by locality and need to be checked before a deck is designed.

A choice between one large deck and two or more smaller decks may be influenced by code limitations, although the choice is more likely to be based on orientation, view, prevailing winds, steepness of the site, or anticipated desires of the owner.

Deciding deck location goes a long way toward determining the type of deck but leaves a wide choice in design. Where wood is selected as the deck material, there are many design considerations that can contribute to deck durability and enhance the owner's enjoyment of this outdoor living area.

Planning a deck during the design of the house is certainly an advantage because it can then become an outdoor extension of the living or family room. It can also be designed as an outdoor portion of the dining room or kitchen with access through sliding doors or other openings. It is also desirable to take advantage of prevailing breezes with space for both sun and shade areas during the day. Sun shades can be used as a substitute for the natural shade provided by trees.

Providing a deck for an existing house is sometimes more difficult because the rooms may not be located to provide easy access to a deck. However, introduction of a new doorway in the house and a pleasant walkway to the deck area may provide a satisfactory solution to even the most difficult problem.

Table 1. — Broad classification of woods according to characteristics and properties[1]

Kind of wood	Working and behavior characteristics							Strength properties			
	Hardness	Freedom from warping	Ease of working	Paint holding	Nail holding	Decay resistance of heartwood	Proportion of heartwood	Bending strength	Stiffness	Strength as a post	Freedom from pitch
Ash	A	B	C	C	A	C	C	A	A	A	A
Western red cedar	C	A	A	A	C	A	A	C	C	B	A
Cypress	B	B	B	A	B	A	B	B	B	B	A
Douglas-fir, larch	B	B	B-C	C	A	B	A	A	A	A	B
Gum	B	C	B	C	A	B	B	B	A	B	A
Hemlock, white fir[2]	B-C	B	B	C	C	C	C	B	A	B	A
Soft pines[3]	C	A	A	A	C	C	B	C	C	C	B
Southern pine	B	B	B	C	A	B	C	A	A	A	C
Poplar	C	A	B	A	B	C	B	B	B	B	A
Redwood	B	A	B	A	B	A	A	B	B	A	A
Spruce	C	A-B	B	B	B	C	C	B	B	B	A

[1] A — among the woods relatively high in the particular respect listed; B — among woods intermediate in that respect; C — among woods relatively low in that respect. Letters do not refer to lumber grades.

[2] Includes west coast and eastern hemlocks.

[3] Includes the western and northeastern pines.

Material Selection

General

Although wood and wood products are the primary materials used in the construction of exposed decks, other materials such as fastenings and finishes are also important. Footings used to anchor the posts which support the deck proper are usually concrete. The proper combinations of all materials with good construction details will insure a deck which will provide years of pleasure.

In addition to the information contained in this manual and selected references, further data on the use of wood can be obtained from many wood trade associations, universities, and wood research laboratories, a few of which are included in the following list:

American Institute of Timber Construction
Englewood, Colorado 80110

American Plywood Association
Tacoma, Washington 98401

American Wood Preservers Bureau
Arlington, Virginia 22206

American Wood Preservers Institute
McLean, Virginia 22101

California Redwood Association
San Francisco, California 94111

National Forest Products Association
Washington, D. C. 20036

Southern Forest Products Association
Metairie, Louisiana 70002

U. S. Forest Products Laboratory
Madison, Wisconsin 53705

Western Wood Products Association
Portland, Oregon 97204

These organizations should always be considered as sources of specific information. However, it is the purpose of this manual to provide general guides to the proper construction of outdoor wood decks and related units. Illustrations of "poor" as well as "good" practices will be included in many instances.

Lumber Species and Characteristics

Many lumber species will provide good service in a wood deck. However, some are more adequate for the purpose than others. To select lumber wisely, one must first single out the key requirements of the job. Then it is relatively easy to check the properties of the different wood to see which ones meet these requirements. For example, beams or joists require wood species that are high in bending strength or stiffness; wide boards in railings or fences may best be species that warp little; posts and similar members that are exposed to long wet periods should be heartwood of species with high decay resistance. Species information is included in Agriculture Information Bulletin No. 311, Selection and Use of Wood Products for Home and Farm Buildings (3). That bulletin lists major items of construction with usual requirements and the species which best combine these requirements. As an example:

DECKING AND OUTDOOR STEPPING

Usual requirements: High decay resistance, non-splintering, good stiffness, strength, wear resistance, and freedom from warping. Woods with heartwood that combine these requirements from a high to a good degree include — cypress, white oak, locust, Douglas-fir, western larch, redwood, cedar, and southern pine.

The classification of woods commonly used in the United States according to their characteristics is given in table 1. Follow the recommendations in this table in selecting wood for a specific use in the outdoor structure.

Plywood is a wood product adaptable for use in wood decks and is often recommended for solid deck coverings . A listing of the five species groups used in the manufacture of softwood plywood is included in U. S. Product Standard PS 1-66 (10). In general, those species of interest for decks are grouped as shown in tables 1, 2, and 3, except that western red cedar, sugar pine, eastern white pine, and Engelmann spruce are excluded from group 3 for plywood and placed in group 4.

Plywood is made in two types — Exterior and Interior. Only Exterior type is recommended where any surface or edge is permanently exposed to the weather. Interior type plywood, even when made with exterior glue and protected on the top surface, is not recommended for such exposures.

Lumber sizes. — The size of lumber is normally based on green sawn sizes. When the lumber has been dried and surfaced, the finish size (thickness and width) is somewhat less than the sawn size.

The following lumber sizes are those established by the American Lumber Standards Committee.

Nominal (inches)	Dry (inches)	Green (inches)
1	3/4	25/32
2	1-1/2	1-9/16
4	3-1/2	3-9/16
6	5-1/2	5-5/8
8	7-1/4	7-1/2
10	9-1/4	9-1/2
12	11-1/4	11-1/2

For example, a nominal 2 by 4 would have a surfaced dry size of 1½ by 3½ inches at a maximum moisture content of 19 percent.

Moisture content of wood during fabrication and assembly of a wood frame structure is important. Ideally, it should be about the same moisture content it reaches in service. If green or partially dried wood is used, wood members usually shrink, resulting in poorly fitting joints and loose fastenings after drying has occurred.

Although not as important for exterior use as for interior use, the moisture content of lumber used and exposed to exterior conditions should be considered. The average moisture content of wood exposed to the weather varies with the season, but kiln dried or air dried lumber best fits the mid-range of moisture contents that wood reaches in use.

Plywood Specifications

For solid deck applications with direct exposure to the weather, plywood marked C-C Plugged Exterior, or Underlayment Exterior (C-C Plugged) may be specified. Higher grades, such as A-C or B-C Exterior, may also be used. These grades coated with a high performance wearing surface are commonly used for residential deck areas.

High Density Overlay (HDO) plywood having a hard, phenolic-resin impregnated fiber surface is often used for boat decks with a screened, skid-resistant finish specified. HDO may be painted with standard deck-type paints, if desired, but is usually used without further finish.

Medium Density Overlay (MDO) plywood having a softer resin-fiber overlay requires either a high-performance deck paint, or an elastomeric deck coating system, depending on the intended use.

For premium deck construction, Plyron (plywood with a tempered hardboard face) may be used in conjunction with an elastomeric deck coating.

Plywood specifications for decks are summarized in table 6.

Decay Resistance of Wood

Every material normally used in construction has its distinctive way of deteriorating under adverse conditions. With wood it is decay. Wood will never decay if kept continuously dry (at less than 20-percent moisture content). Because open decks and other outdoor components are exposed to wetting and drying conditions, good drainage, flashings, and similar protective measures are more important in decks than in structures fully protected by a roof.

To provide good performance of wood under exposed conditions, one or more of the following measures should be taken:
  (1) Use the heartwood of a decay-resistant species.
  (2) Use wood that has been given a good preservative treatment.

(3) Use details which do not trap moisture and which allow easy drainage. (A combination of (1) and (3), for example, is considered adequate, and (2) is satisfactory alone, but usually at increased cost if pressure treatment is used, or at the expense of increased maintenance if dip or soak treatments are used. Detailing that allows quick drying is always desirable and will be emphasized here).

Frequently, it is cheaper and easier to use a good connection design than to use an inferior detail with a decay-resistant wood.

Figure 4. — Solid carpeted decks harmonize interior and exterior living areas.

Treatments, Finishes, and Coverings for Decks

Preservative Treatments

The best treatment of wood to assure long life under severe conditions is a pressure preservative treatment (9). However, most of the wood parts of a deck are exposed only to moderate conditions except at joints and connections. There are two general methods of preservatively treating wood, (a) pressure processes applied commercially according to American Wood-Preservers' Association (AWPA) standards (2) which provide lasting protection; (b) non-pressure processes which normally penetrate the ends and a thin layer of the outer surfaces and require frequent maintenance. The non-pressure processes refer to treatments with water-repellent wood preservatives.

Two general types of preservatives are recommended for severe exterior conditions: (a) oils, such as creosote, or pentachlorophenol in oil or liquified gas carriers, and (b) non-leachable salts, such as the chromated copper arsenates or ammoniacal copper arsenite applied as water solutions. Both types are adequately described in the AWPA book of standards (2).

Poles and posts (severe conditions). — Treatment of poles and posts which are in contact with the soil should comply with the latest Federal specification TT-W-571i or with AWPA standards (2). Insist that the wood material you buy for these purposes has been treated according to these recommended practices.

Lumber and timber for ground or water contact (severe conditions). — Wood used under severe conditions such as ground contact may be pressure treated as recommended for poles and posts. However, if cleanliness or paintability is a factor, creosote or pentachloro-phenol in heavy oil should not be used. AWPA standards for non-leachable water-borne preservatives and pentachlorophenol in light or volatile petroleum solvents should be selected (2).

Wood not in contact with ground. — Where preservative treatment is desirable because the more decay-resistant woods are not available, the use of a more easily applied, less expensive but less effective non-pressure treatment may be considered for joints, connections, and other critical areas. A pentachlorophenol solution with a water repellent is one of the more effective materials of this type. It is available at most lumber or paint dealers as a clear, water-repellent preservative which should perform in accordance with Federal specification TT-W-572. Sears, Roebuck & Company's "Wood Tox" is one of many products available.[1]

These materials should be applied by soaking, dipping, or flooding so that end grain, machine cuts, and any existing checks in the wood are well penetrated. Dipping each end of all exterior framing material in water-repellent preservative is recommended, and this should be done after all cutting and drilling is completed. Drilled holes can be easily treated by squirting preservative from an oil can with a long spout. Dry wood absorbs more of these materials than partially dry wood and, consequently, is better protected.

---

[1] *Trade names are used only for the information and convenience of readers. Such use does not constitute endorsement by the U. S. Dept. of Agriculture of any product to the exclusion of others that may be suitable.*

Plywood decks. — Preservative treatments for plywood decks are covered by the same standards as those for lumber and may be applied by pressure or superficial soaking or dipping. Several types of treatments perform well on plywood; but some deck applications require specific treatments, and the compatibility of the treatment with finish materials should always be checked.

Light, oil-borne preservatives and water-borne preservatives, such as those recommended for lumber, should be used when a clean, odorless, and paintable treatment is required. For maximum service from plywood decks, these preservatives should be pressure applied.

Exterior Finishes for Wood

Exterior finishes which might be considered for wood components exposed to the weather include natural finishes, penetrating stains, and paints. In general, natural finishes containing a water repellent and a preservative are preferred over paint for exposed flat surfaces. The natural finishes penetrate the wood and are easily renewed, but paint forms a surface film that may rupture under repeated wetting and drying. Exposed flat surfaces of decks, railings, and stairways are more vulnerable to paint film rupture than are vertical sidewall surfaces. Therefore, a completely satisfactory siding paint may not be suitable for a deck.

Natural finishes (lightly pigmented) are often used for exposed wood decks, railings, and stairways, not only because they can be easily renewed but because they enhance the natural color and grain of the wood. Such finishes can be obtained in many colors from a local paint dealer. Light colors are better for deck surfaces subject to traffic, as they show the least contrast in grain color as wear occurs and appearance is maintained longer.

One type of natural finish contains paraffin wax, zinc stearate, penta concentrate, linseed oil, mineral spirits, and tinting colors. Such finishes are manufactured by many leading producers of wood stains and are generally available from paint or lumber dealers. Formulas for several finishes of this type are also outlined in a report of the U. S. Forest Laboratory (7).

Penetrating stains (heavily pigmented) for rough and weathered wood may be used on the large sawn members such as beams and posts. These are similar to the natural finishes just described but contain less oil and more pigment. They are also produced by many companies.

Paint is one of the most widely used finishes for wood. When applied properly over a paintable surface with an initial water-repellent preservative treatment, followed by prime and finish coats, paint is a highly desirable finish for outdoor structures or as an accent color when used with natural finishes. Exposed flat surfaces with end or side joints are difficult to protect with a paint coating unless there is no shrinking or swelling of the wood to rupture the paint film. A crack in the paint film allows water to get beneath the film where it is hard to remove by drying. Retention of such moisture can result in eventual decay. Proper application methods and materials have been published by the U. S. Forest Products Laboratory (8).

Good painting practices include an initial application of water repellent preservative. After allowing two sunny days for drying of the preservative, a prime coat is applied. This can consist of a linseed oil-base paint with pigments that do not contain zinc oxide.

The finish coats can contain zinc oxide pigment and can be of the linseed oil, alkyd, or latex type. Two coats should be used for best results. A three-coat paint job with good-quality paint may last as long as 10 years, when the film is not ruptured by excessive shrinking or swelling of the wood.

Coverings and Coatings for Plywood Decks

Tough, skid-resistant, elastomeric coatings are available for plywood deck wearing surfaces. These coatings include liquid neoprene, neoprene/Hypalon, and silicone- or rubber-based materials. Plywood joints for these systems are usually sealed with a high performance caulk such as a silicone or Thiokol (silicone caulks require a primer). Joints may also be covered with a synthetic reinforcing tape, prior to application of the final surface coat, when an elastomeric coating system is used.

Silicone or Thiokol caulks are applied to 1/4-inch gaps between plywood panels over some type of filler or "backer" material — such as a foam rod. The caulk "bead" is normally about one-fourth inch in diameter. An alternate method is to bevel the panel edges first, then fill the joint with the caulk before the finish coating is applied.

For a premium quality joint, reinforcing tape is sometimes applied as a flashing over sealed joints. Reinforcing tape can also be used over cant strips at wall-to-deck corner areas and over unsealed plywood joints. For these applications, the tape flashing is embedded in a base coat of the elastomeric deck coating. Specific installation procedures and recommendations are readily available from manufacturers of the various deck coating systems and from the American Plywood Association. Their installation recommendations should be carefully followed.

Where plywood must be installed under wet conditions, the primer or first coat may be applied in the factory or under shelter at the site prior to installation of the panels. In general, the first coat of coating systems for plywood should be applied to a dry, fresh wood surface. Where preservatives are used, the surface should be scraped or sanded to remove any residue produced by the preservative before the prime coat is applied. Finish coats of most systems require a dry clean surface, for best results.

If outdoor carpeting is to be used on plywood exposed to the weather, it is advisable to use pressure preservative treated plywood, with the underside well ventilated, for both low and elevated decks. Since carpeting is relatively new as an exterior surface material, specific information on its long-term performance when used on plywood under severe exposure is not available. Carpet may be readily applied to untreated plywood deck areas that are not subject to repeated wetting.

Canvas is sometimes used as a wearing surface on plywood. It should be installed with a waterproof adhesive, under dry conditions. A canvas surface well fused to the plywood may be painted with regular deck paints.

Design Recommendations

Framing Spans and Sizes

The allowable spans for decking, joists, and beams and the size of posts depend not only on the size, grade, and spacing of the members but also on the species. Species such as Douglas-fir, southern pine, and western larch allow greater spans than some of the less dense pines, cedars, and redwood, for example. Normally, deck members are designed for about the same load as the floors in a dwelling.

The arrangement of the structural members can vary somewhat because of orientation of the deck, position of the house, slope of the lot, etc. However, basically, the beams are supported by the posts (anchored to footings) which in turn support the floor joists (fig. 5). The deck boards are then fastened to the joists. When beams are spaced more closely together, the joists can be eliminated if the deck boards are thick enough to span between the beams. Railings are located around the perimeter of the deck if required for safety (low-level decks are often constructed without edge railings). When the deck is fastened to the house in some manner, the deck is normally rigid enough to eliminate the need for post bracing. In high free-standing decks, the use of post bracing is good practice.

Post sizes. — Common sizes for wood posts used in supporting beams and floor framing for wood decks are 4 by 4, 4 by 6, and 6 by 6 inches. The size of the post required is based on the span and spacing of the beams, the load, and the height of the post. Most decks are designed for a live load of 40 pounds per square foot with an additional allowance of 10 pounds per square foot for the weight of the material. The suggested sizes of posts required for various heights under several beam spans and spacings are listed in table 2. Under normal conditions, the minimum dimension of the post should be the same as the beam width to simplify the method of fastening the two together. Thus a 4- by 8-inch (on edge) beam might use a 4- by 4-inch or a 4- by 6-inch post depending on the height, etc.

Beam spans. — The nominal sizes of beams for various spacings and spans are listed in table 3. These sizes are based on such species as Douglas-fir, southern pine, and western larch for one group, western hemlock and white fir for a second group, and the soft pines, cedars, spruces, and redwood for a third group. Lumber grade is No. 2 or Better.

Joist spans. — The approximate allowable spans for joists used in outdoor decks are listed in table 4 — both for the denser species of Group 1 and the less dense species of Groups 2 and 3. These spans are based on strength (40 pounds per square foot live load plus 10 pounds per square foot dead load) with deflection not exceeding 1/360 of span.

Deck board spans. — Deck boards are mainly used in 2-inch thickness and in widths of 3 and 4 inches. Because deck boards are spaced, spans are normally based on the width of each board as well as its thickness. (Roof decking, with tongue and groove edges and laid up tight, has greater allowable spans than spaced boards.) Decking can also be made of 2- by 3-inch or 2- by 4-inch members placed on edge, or of 1- by 4-inch boards. Deck boards are listed in table 5.

Plywood decks. — Spans for plywood decks are shown in table 6.

Fasteners

The strength and utility of any wood struc-

11

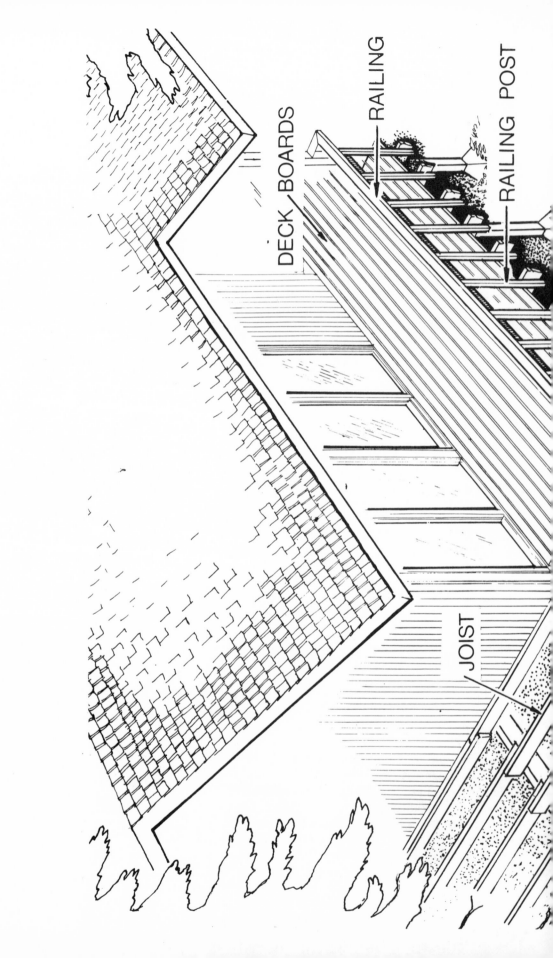

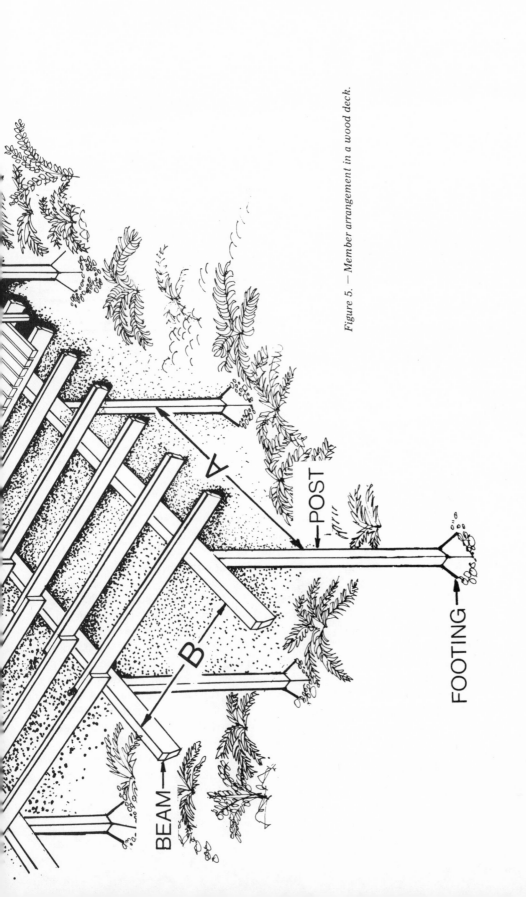

Figure 5. — *Member arrangement in a wood deck.*

POST

BEAM

FOOTING

A

B

Table 2. — Minimum post sizes (wood beam supports)[1]

Species group[2]	Post size (in.)	Load area[3] beam spacing x post spacing (sq. ft.)									
		36	48	60	72	84	96	108	120	132	144
1	4x4	Up to 12-ft. heights——→					Up to 10-ft. heights→		Up to 8-ft. heights→		
	4x6						Up to 12-ft. heights——→			Up to 10-ft.→	
	6x6									Up to 12-ft.→	
2	4x4	Up to 12-ft.→		Up to 10-ft. hts.——→		Up to 8-ft. heights———————→					
	4x6			Up to 12-ft. hts.——→		Up to 10-ft. heights———→					
	6x6					Up to 12-ft. heights———————————→					
3	4x4	Up to 12'	Up to 10'——→		Up to 8-ft. hts.——→		Up to 6-ft. heights————————→				
	4x6		Up to 12'——→		Up to 10-ft. hts.——→		Up to 8-ft. heights————————→				
	6x6				Up to 12-ft. heights————————————————→						

[1] *Based on 40 p.s.f. deck live load plus 10 p.s.f. dead load. Grade is Standard and Better for 4- x 4-inch posts and No. 1 and Better for larger sizes.*

[2] *Group 1 — Douglas-fir-larch and southern pine; Group 2 — Hem-fir and Douglas-fir south; Group 3 — Western pines and cedars, redwood, and spruces.*

[3] *Example: If the beam supports are spaced 8 feet, 6 inches, on center and the posts are 11 feet, 6 inches, on center, then the load area is 98. Use next larger area 108.*

ture or component are in great measure dependent upon the fastenings used to hold the parts together. The most common wood fasteners are nails and spikes, followed by screws, lag screws, bolts, and metal connectors and straps of various shapes. An important factor for outdoor use of fasteners is the finish selected. Metal fasteners should be rust-proofed in some manner or made of rust-resistant metals. Galvanized and cadmium plated finishes are the most common. Aluminum, stainless steel, copper, brass, and other rust-proof fasteners are also satisfactory. The most successful for such species as redwood are hot-dip galvanized, aluminum, or stainless steel fasteners. These prevent staining of the wood under exposed conditions. A rusted nail, washer, or bolt head is not only unsightly but difficult to remove and replace. They are often a factor in the loss of strength of the connection.

Among the nails, smooth shank nails often lose their holding power when exposed to wetting and drying cycles. The best assurance of a high retained withdrawal resistance is the use of a deformed shank nail or spike. The two general types most satisfactory are (a) the annular grooved (ring shank) and (b) the spirally grooved nail (fig. 6). The value of such a nail or spike is its capacity to retain withdrawal resistance even after repeated wetting and drying cycles. Such nails should be used for the construction of exposed units if screws, lag screws, or bolts are not used.

The following tabulation lists the sizes of common nails ordinarily used in construction of outdoor wood structures. (Note: Sinker and

14

Table 3. — Minimum beam sizes and spans[1]

Species group[2] 1

Beam size (in.)	Spacing between beams[3] (ft.)								
	4	5	6	7	8	9	10	11	12
4x6	Up to 6-ft. spans →		Up to 7'						
3x8	Up to 8-ft. →		Up to 6-ft. spans →						
4x8	Up to 10'	Up to 9'	Up to 8'	Up to 9' →		Up to 6-ft. spans			
3x10	Up to 11'	Up to 10'	Up to 9'	Up to 8'	Up to 7' →		Up to 6-ft.		
4x10	Up to 12'	Up to 11'	Up to 10'	Up to 9'	Up to 8'	Up to 8' →		Up to 7-ft.	
3x12		Up to 12'	Up to 11'	Up to 10'	Up to 9'	Up to 8-ft. spans →			
4x12			Up to 12'	Up to 11'	Up to 10'	Up to 10'	Up to 9' →		Up to 9-ft. spans
6x10				Up to 12'	Up to 11'	Up to 10'	Up to 10-ft. →		Up to 10-ft. spans
6x12					Up to 12'	Up to 12-ft. spans →			Up to 12-ft. spans

Species group[2] 2

Beam size (in.)	4	5	6	7	8	9	10	11	12
4x6	Up to 6-ft. →		Up to 6-ft.						
3x8	Up to 7-ft. →		Up to 6-ft. →		Up to 6-ft.				
4x8	Up to 9'	Up to 8'	Up to 7'	Up to 7-ft. →		Up to 6-ft. spans →			Up to 6'
3x10	Up to 10'	Up to 9'	Up to 8'	Up to 8'	Up to 7' →		Up to 6-ft. spans →		
4x10	Up to 11'	Up to 10'	Up to 9'	Up to 9'	Up to 8-ft. →		Up to 7-ft. spans →		
3x12	Up to 12'	Up to 11'	Up to 10'	Up to 10'	Up to 8-ft.	Up to 9'	Up to 7-ft. spans →		
4x12		Up to 12'	Up to 11'	Up to 11'	Up to 10'	Up to 9-ft. →		Up to 8-ft. spans →	
6x10			Up to 12'	Up to 11'	Up to 10-ft. →		Up to 9-ft. spans →		
6x12				Up to 12-ft. spans →		Up to 12-ft. spans	Up to 11' →		Up to 10'

Species group[2] 3

Beam size (in.)	4	5	6	7	8	9	10	11	12
4x6	Up to 6'		Up to 6-ft.						
3x8	Up to 7'	Up to 6-ft. →							
4x8	Up to 8'	Up to 7'	Up to 6-ft. →						
3x10	Up to 9'	Up to 8'	Up to 7'	Up to 6-ft. spans →			Up to 6-ft. spans		
4x10	Up to 10'	Up to 9'	Up to 8'	Up to 8'	Up to 7-ft. →		Up to 7-ft. spans		
3x12	Up to 11'	Up to 10'	Up to 9'	Up to 8'	Up to 7-ft. spans →			Up to 6-ft. spans	
4x12	Up to 12'	Up to 11'	Up to 10'	Up to 9'	Up to 9'	Up to 8' →		Up to 7-ft.	
6x10		Up to 12'	Up to 11'	Up to 10'	Up to 9-ft. →		Up to 8-ft. spans →		
6x12			Up to 12-ft. →		Up to 11-ft.		Up to 10-ft. →		Up to 8'

[1] Beams are on edge. Spans are center to center distances between posts or supports. (Based on 40 p.s.f. deck live load plus 10 p.s.f. dead load. Grade is No. 2 or Better; No. 2, medium grain southern pine.)

[2] Group 1 — Douglas fir-larch and southern pine; Group 2 — Hem-fir and Douglas-fir south; Group 3 — Western pines and cedars, redwood, and spruces.

[3] Example: If the beams are 9 feet, 8 inches apart and the species is Group 2, use the 10-ft. column; 3x10 up to 6-ft. spans, 4x10 or 3x12 up to 7-ft. spans, 4x12 or 6x10 up to 9-ft. spans, 6x12 up to 11-ft. spans.

Table 4. — Maximum allowable spans for deck joists[1]

Species group[2]	Joist size (inches)	Joist spacing (inches)		
		16	24	32
1	2x6	9'-9"	7'-11"	6'-2"
	2x8	12'-10"	10'-6"	8'-1"
	2x10	16'-5"	13'-4"	10'-4"
2	2x6	8'-7"	7'-0"	5'-8"
	2x8	11'-4"	9'-3"	7'-6"
	2x10	14'-6"	11'-10"	9'-6"
3	2x6	7'-9"	6'-2"	5'-0"
	2x8	10'-2"	8'-1"	6'-8"
	2x10	13'-0"	10'-4"	8'-6"

[1] Joists are on edge. Spans are center to center distances between beams or supports. Based on 40 p.s.f. deck live loads plus 10 p.s.f. dead load. Grade is No. 2 or Better; No. 2 medium grain southern pine.

[2] Group 1 — Douglas-fir-larch and southern pine; Group 2 — Hem-fir and Douglas-fir south; Group 3 — Western pines and cedars, redwood, and spruces.

Table 5. — Maximum allowable spans for spaced deck boards[1]

Species group[2]	Maximum allowable span (inches)[3]					
	Laid flat				Laid on edge	
	1 x 4	2 x 2	2 x 3	2 x 4	2 x 3	2 x 4
1	16	60	60	60	90	144
2	14	48	48	48	78	120
3	12	42	42	42	66	108

[1] These spans are based on the assumption that more than one floor board carries normal loads. If concentrated loads are a rule, spans should be reduced accordingly.

[2] Group 1 — Douglas-fir-larch and southern pine; Group 2 — Hem-fir and Douglas-fir south; Group 3 — Western pines and cedars, redwood, and spruces.

[3] Based on Construction grade or Better (Select Structural, Appearance, No. 1 or No. 2).

Table 6. — Recommended grades, minimum thicknesses, and nailing details for various spans and species groups of plywood decking[1]

Plywood species group[2]	Panel thicknesses in inches[3] [4]			
	For maximum spacings between supports (inches)			
	16	20	24	32 or 48
1	1/2	5/8	3/4	1-1/8
2 & 3	5/8	3/4	7/8	1-1/8
4	3/4	7/8	1	[5]

[1] *Recommended thicknesses are based on Underlayment Exterior (C-C Plugged) grade. Higher grades, such as A-C or B-C Exterior, may be used. 19/32-inch plywood may be substituted for 5/8-inch and 23/32-inch for 3/4-inch.*

[2] *Plywood species groups are approximately the same but not identical to those shown for lumber in tables 2-5. Therefore, in selecting plywood, one should be guided by the group number stamped on the panel.*

[3] *Edges of panels shall be T&G or supported by blocking.*

[4] *Nailing details: Size — 6d deformed shank nails, except 8d for 7/8-inch or 1-1/8-inch plywood on spans 24 to 48 inches. Spacing — 6 inches along panel edges, 10 inches along intermediate supports (6 inches for 48-inch on center supports). Corrosion resistant nails are recommended where nail heads are to be exposed. Nails should be set 1/16 inch (1/8 inch for 1 1/8-inch plywood).*

[5] *Not permitted.*

cooler nails are one-eighth to one-fourth inch shorter.)

	Nail size (penny)	Nail length (inches)
	4	1-1/2
	6	2
	7	2-1/4
	8	2-1/2
	10	3
	12	3-1/4
	16	3-1/2
	20	4
Usually classed as spikes	30	4-1/2
	40	5
	50	5-1/2
	60	6

Wood screws may be used if cost is not a factor in areas where nails are normally specified. Wood screws retain their withdrawal resistance to a great extent under adverse conditions. They are also superior to nails when endgrain fastening must be used. Because of their larger diameter, screw length need not be as great as a deformed shank nail. The flathead screw is best for exposed surfaces because it does not extend beyond the surface (fig. 7), and the oval head protrudes less than the round head screw. This is an important factor in the construction of tables and benches. The use of a lead hole about three-fourths the diameter of the screw is good practice especially in the denser woods to prevent splitting. Screws should always be turned in their full length and not driven part way. The new variable speed

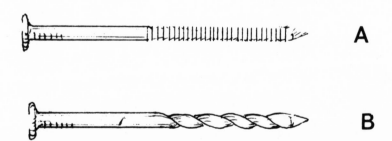

A

B

Figure 6. — Deformed shank nails. A — annular grooved (ring shank); B — spirally grooved.

drills (with a screwdriver) are excellent for applying screws.

Lag screws are commonly used to fasten a relatively thick, such as 2- by 6-inch, member to a thicker member (3-or-more-inch) where a through bolt cannot be used. Lead holes must be used, and the lag screw turned in its entire length. Use a large washer under the head. Lead holes for the threaded portion should be about two-thirds the diameter of the lag screw for the softer woods such as redwood or cedar, and three-fourths the diameter for the dense hardwoods and for such species as Douglas-fir. The lead hole for the unthreaded shank of the lag screw should be the same diameter as that of the lag screw.

Bolts are one of the most rigid fasteners in a simple form. They may be used for small connections such as railings-to-posts and for large members when combined with timber connectors. The two types of bolts most commonly used in light frame construction are the carriage bolt and the machine bolt (fig. 8). When obtainable, the step bolt is preferred over the carriage bolt because of its larger head diameter.

The carriage bolt is normally used without a washer under the head. A squared section at the bolt head resists turning as it is tightened. Washers should always be used under the head of the machine bolt and under the nut of both types. Bolt holes should be the exact diameter of the bolt. When a bolt-fastened member is loaded, such as a beam to a post, the bearing strength of the wood under the bolt is important as well as the strength of the bolt. A larger diameter bolt or several smaller diameter bolts may be used when the softer woods are involved. Crushing of wood under the head of a carriage bolt or under the washer of any bolt should always be avoided. The use of larger washers and a washer under the carriage bolt head is advisable when the less dense wood species are used.

For connections involving specific design in large members with split ring and similar connectors, the 1966 Timber Construction Manual of the American Institute of Timber Construction (1) or the Forest Products Laboratory Wood Handbook (9) should be consulted.

Miscellaneous fastening methods in addition to the nail, screw, and bolt are also used for fastening wood members together, or to other materials. Although split ring connectors and similar fasteners are normally used for large beams or trusses, other connectors may be used to advantage in the construction of a wood deck. These include metal anchors for connecting posts to concrete footings; angle iron and special connectors for fastening posts to beams; joist hangers and metal strapping for fastening joists to beams; and others. While research has not advanced far enough as yet, the new mastic adhesives are showing promise for field assembly of certain wood members. Such materials used alone or with metal fasteners will likely result in longer-lived connections.

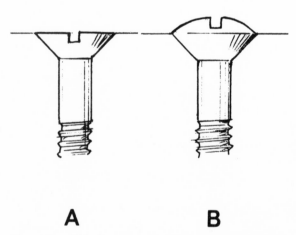

A   **B**

Figure 7. — Wood screws. A — flat head; B — oval head.

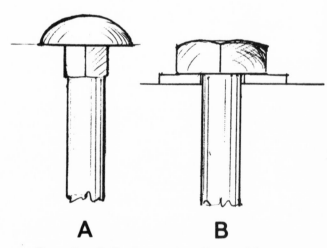

A   **B**

Figure 8. — Bolts. A — carriage; B — machine.

General Rules for Deck Construction

Our experience with exposed deck construction can be summarized in the following general guides for the use of wood and fasteners in outdoor decks.

Guides for Fastener Use

1. Use non-staining fasteners.
2. Always fasten a thinner member to a thicker member (unless clinched nails are used).
   (a) A nail should be long enough to penetrate the receiving member a distance twice the thickness of the thinner member but not less than 1-1/2 inches (i.e., for a 3/4-inch board, the nail should penetrate the receiving member 1-1/2 inches. Use at least a 7-penny nail).
   (b) A screw should be long enough to penetrate the receiving member at least the thickness of the thinner (outside) member but with not less than a 1-inch penetration (i.e., fastening a 3/4-inch member to a 2 by 4 would require a 1-3/4-inch-long screw).
3. To reduce splitting of boards when nailing —
   (a) Blunt the nail point.
   (b) Predrill (three-fourths of nail diameter).
   (c) Use smaller diameter nails and a greater number.
   (d) Use greater spacing between nails.
   (e) Stagger nails in each row.
   (f) Place nails no closer to edge than one-half of the board thickness and no closer to end than the board thickness.

(g) In wide boards (8 inches or more), do not place nails close to edge.
4. Use minimum of two nails per board — i.e., two nails for 4- and 6-inch widths and three nails for 8- and 10-inch widths.
5. Avoid end grain nailing. When unavoidable, use screws or side grain wood cleat adjacent to end grain member (as a post).
6. Lag screw use —
   (a) Use a plain, flat washer under the head.
   (b) Use lead hole and turn in full distance; do not overturn.
   (c) Do not countersink (reduces wood section).
7. Bolt use —
   (a) Use flat washers under nut and head of machine bolts and under nut of carriage bolt. In softer woods, use larger washer under carriage bolt heads.
   (b) Holes to be exact size of bolt diameter.

Guides for Outdoor Wood Use

1. When a wide member is required, use edge grain boards, as they shrink, swell, and cup less than flat grain boards during moisture changes.
2. Do not use wood in direct contact with soil unless members are pressure treated.
3. Provide clearance of wood members (fences, posts, etc.) from plant growth and ground to minimize high moisture content. Bottoms of posts, when supported by piers for example, should be 6 inches above the grade.

4. Use forms of flat members which provide natural drainage (a sloped top of a cap rail, for example).

5. Use rectangular sections with width and thickness as nearly equal as possible, i.e.,

3 by 4 instead of 2 by 6.

6. Dip all ends and points of fabrication in a water-repellent preservative treatment prior to placement.

Figure 9. — Decks expand living areas on steep hillsides with little disturbance of the ground.

Deck Construction

Site Preparation

Grading and drainage. — Site preparation for construction of a wood deck is often less costly than that for a concrete terrace. When the site is steep, it is difficult to grade and to treat the backslopes in preparing a base for the concrete slab. In grading the site for a wood deck, one must normally consider only proper drainage, disturbing the natural terrain as little as possible. Grading should be enough to insure water runoff, usually just a minor leveling of the ground.

Often, absorption of the soil under an open deck with spaced boards will account for a good part of a moderate rainfall. If the deck also serves as a roof for a garage, carport, or living area below, drainage should be treated as a part of the house roof drainage, whether by gutters, downspouts, or drip and drain pockets at the ground level. In such cases, some form of drainage may be required to carry water away from the site and prevent erosion. This can usually be accomplished with drain tile laid in a shallow drainage ditch (fig. 10). Tile should be spaced and joints covered with a strip of asphalt felt before the trench is filled. The tile can lead to a dry well or to a drainage field beyond the site. Perforated cement or plastic tile is also available for this use.

Weed and growth control. — There may also be a need for control of weed growth beneath the deck. Without some control or deterrent, such growth can lead to high moisture content of wood members and subsequent decay hazards where decks are near the grade. Common methods for such control consist of (a) the application of a weed killer to the plants or (b) the use of a membrane such as 4- or 6-mil polyethylene or 30-pound asphalt saturated felt.

Such coverings should be placed just before the deck boards are laid. Stones, bricks, or other permanent means of anchoring the membranes in place should be used around the perimeter and in any interior surface variations which may be present. A few holes should be punched in the covering so that a good share of the rain will not run off and cause erosion.

Footings

Some type of footing is required to support the posts or poles which transfer the deck loads to the ground. In simplest form, the bottom of a treated pole and the friction of the earth around the pole provide this support. More commonly, however, some type of masonry, usually concrete, is used as a footing upon which the poles or posts rest. Several footing systems are normally used, some more preferred than others.

Footings for posts below grade. — Footings required for support of vertical members such as wood poles or posts must be designed to carry the load of the deck superstructure (11). In a simple form, the design includes the use of pressure-treated posts or poles embedded to a depth which provides sufficient bearing and rigidity (fig. 11). This may require a depth of 3 to 5 feet or more, depending on the exposed pole height and applied loads. This type is perhaps more commonly used for pole structures such as storage sheds or barns. In areas where frost is a problem, such as in the Northern States, an embedment depth of 4 feet is commonly a minimum. But a lesser depth may be adequate in warmer climates. Soil should be well-tamped around the pole.

Concrete footings below the surface are normally used for treated posts or poles. Two

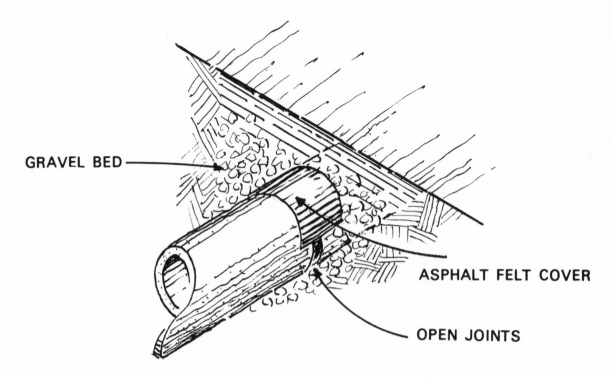

GRAVEL BED

ASPHALT FELT COVER

OPEN JOINTS

CEMENT OR TILE DRAIN PIPE

Figure 10. — Drain tile.

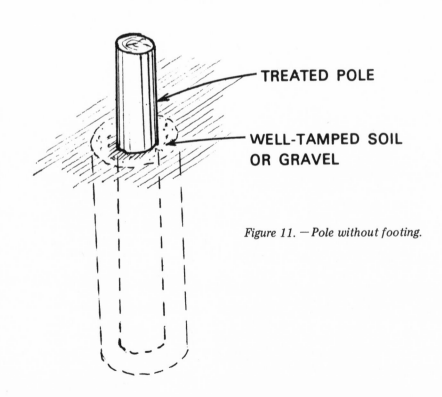

TREATED POLE

WELL-TAMPED SOIL
OR GRAVEL

Figure 11. — Pole without footing.

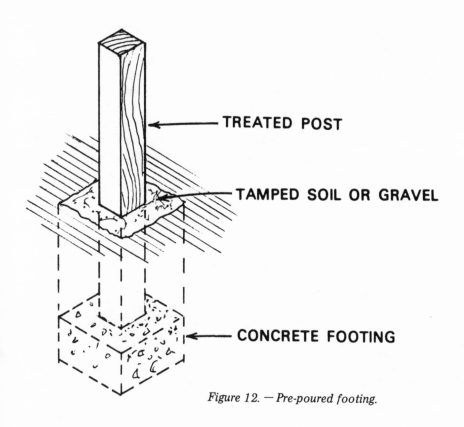

TREATED POST

TAMPED SOIL OR GRAVEL

CONCRETE FOOTING

Figure 12. — Pre-poured footing.

such types may be used. The first consists of a pre-poured footing upon which the wood members rest (fig. 12). Embedment depth should be only enough to provide lateral resistance, usually 2 to 3 feet. The exception is in cold climates where frost may penetrate to a depth of 4 feet or more. Minimum size for concrete footings in normal soils should be 12 by 12 by 8 inches. Where spacing of the poles is over about 6 feet, 20 by 20 by 10 inches or larger sizes are preferred. However, soil capacities should be determined before design.

Another type of below-grade footing is the poured-in-place type shown in fig. 13. In such construction, the poles are pre-aligned, plumbed, and supported above the bottom of the excavated hole. Concrete is then poured below and around the butt end of the pole. A minimum thickness of 8 inches of concrete below the bottom of the pole is advisable. Soil may be added above the concrete when necessary for protection in cold weather. Such foot-

ings do not require tamped soil around the pole to provide lateral resistance. All poles or posts embedded in the soil should always be pressure treated for long life.

Footings for posts above grade. — Footings or footing extensions for posts which are entirely exposed above the grade are poured so the top is at least 6 inches above the surrounding soil. When the size of the footing is greater than the post size (which is normal), a pedestal-type extension is often used (fig. 14A). The bottom of the footing should be located below frost level which may require a long pier-type pedestal. A wood form can be used when pouring pedestal (fig. 14B). Made in this manner with extension on each side, it is easily demountable. The use of form nails (double-head) is also satisfactory. Bolts, angle irons, or other post anchorage should be placed when pouring, and anchor bolts or other bond bars should extend into the footing for positive anchorage against uplift.

23

Post-to-Footing Anchorage

The anchorage of supporting posts to footings with top surfaces above grade is important as they should not only resist lateral movement but also uplift stresses which can occur during periods of high winds. These anchorages should be designed for good drainage and freedom from contact of the end-grain of the wood with wet concrete. This is advisable to prevent decay or damage to the bottom of the wood post. It is also important that the post ends be given a dip treatment of water-repellent preservative. Un-fortunately, such features are sometimes lacking in post anchorage. As recommended for nails, screws, bolts, and other fastenings, all metal anchors should be galvanized or treated in some manner to resist corrosion.

Poor design includes an embedded wood block as a fastening member with the post toe-nailed in place (fig. 15A). This is generally poor practice even when the block has been pressure treated, as moisture can accumulate in the post bottom.

Another poor practice is shown in fig. 15B.

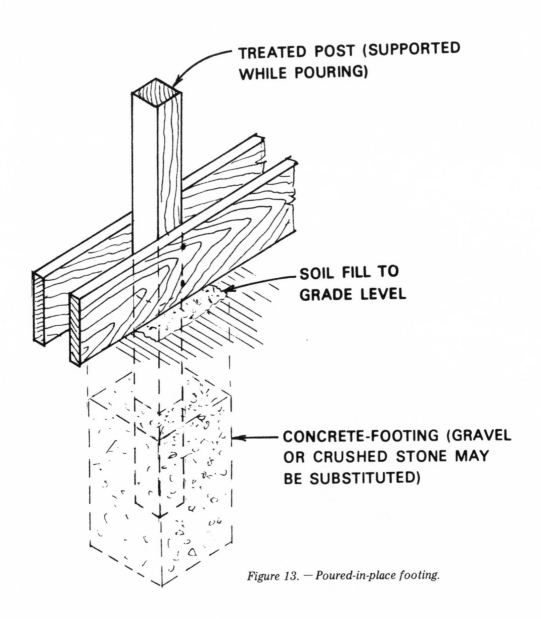

TREATED POST (SUPPORTED WHILE POURING)

SOIL FILL TO GRADE LEVEL

CONCRETE-FOOTING (GRAVEL OR CRUSHED STONE MAY BE SUBSTITUTED)

Figure 13. — Poured-in-place footing.

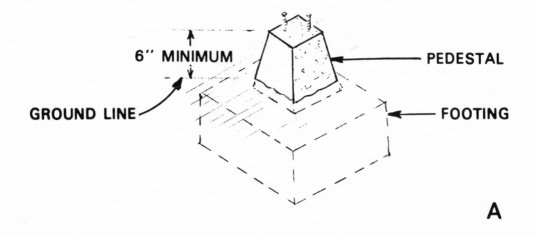

6" MINIMUM

GROUND LINE

PEDESTAL

FOOTING

A

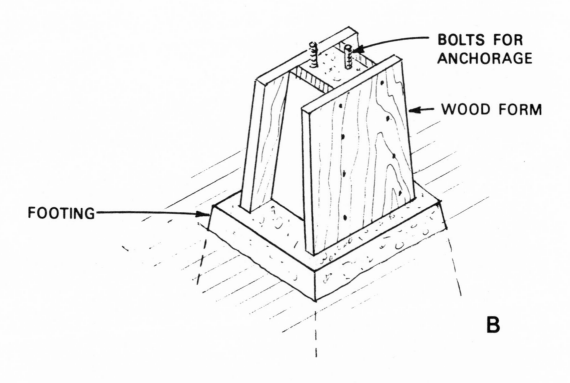

BOLTS FOR
ANCHORAGE

WOOD FORM

FOOTING

B

Figure 14. — Pedestal footing extension. A — pedestal for post; B — form used for pouring.

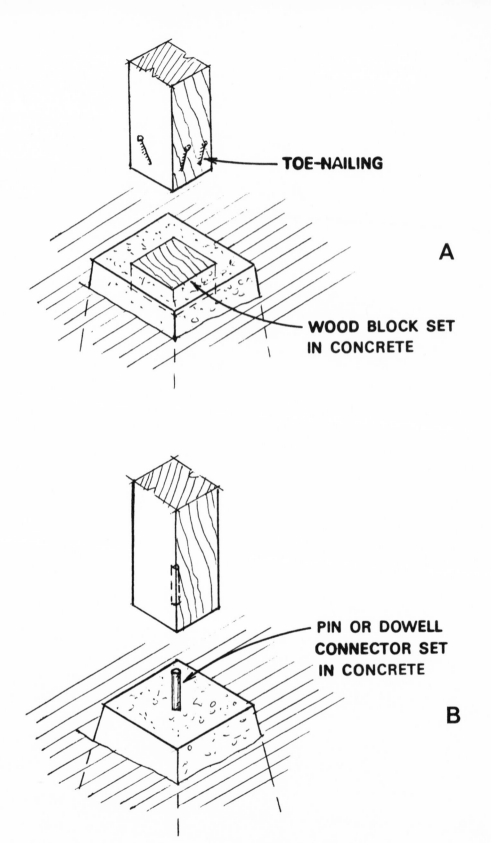

TOE-NAILING

WOOD BLOCK SET
IN CONCRETE

A

PIN OR DOWELL
CONNECTOR SET
IN CONCRETE

B

Figure 15. — Post-to-footing anchorage. A and B — poor practice.

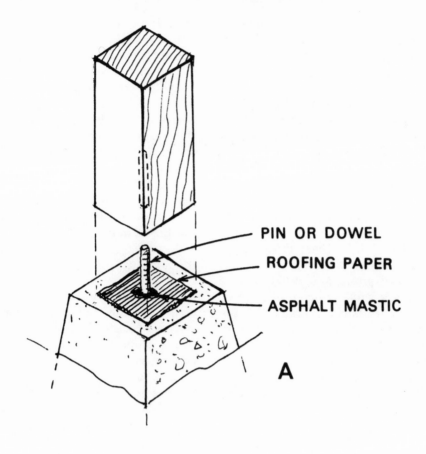

PIN OR DOWEL

ROOFING PAPER

ASPHALT MASTIC

A

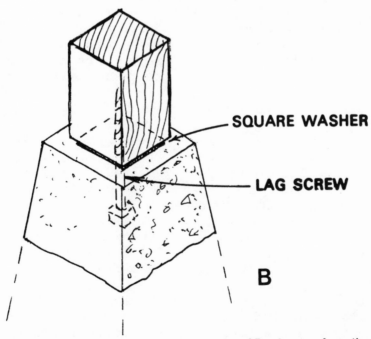

SQUARE WASHER

LAG SCREW

B

Figure 16. — Post-to-footing anchorage. A and B — improved practice.

The bottom of the post is in direct contact with the concrete footing which can result in moisture absorption. Although the pin anchor resists lateral movement, it has little uplift resistance.

Better design of fig. 16A is a slight improvement over fig. 15B as a heavy roofing paper and roofing mastic prevents the bottom of the post from absorbing moisture from the concrete footing.

A better system of anchoring small 4- by 4-inch posts is shown in fig. 16B. In such anchorage, a galvanized lag screw is turned into the bottom of the post with a large square washer (about 3- by 3- by 1/4-inch thick for a 4- by 4-inch post) placed for a bearing area. Post is then anchored into a grouted pre-drilled hole or supported in place while concrete is poured. The washer prevents direct contact with the concrete and prevents moisture wicking into the bottom of the post, and the lag screw head provides some uplift resistance.

Good design is an anchorage system for supporting small posts, beams, stair treads, and similar members, utilizing a small steel pipe (galvanized or painted) with a pipe flange at each end (fig. 17A). A welded plate or angle iron can be substituted for the pipe flange (fig. 17B). The pipe flange or plate-to-post connection should be made with large screws or lag screws. The flange can be fastened to the post bottom and turned in place after the concrete is poured (fig. 17A). When an angle iron is used, the entire assembly is poured in place. A good anchor for beams used in low decks is shown in fig. 17C.

Other post anchors can be obtained (or made up) for anchoring wood posts to a masonry base. Such anchors are normally used for solid 4- by 4-inch or larger posts. All are designed to provide lateral as well as uplift resistance. Some means such as a plate or supporting angle is provided to prevent contact of the post with the concrete, thus reducing the chances for decay. All holes drilled into posts for the purpose of anchorage should be flushed with a water-repellent preservative to provide protection. An oil can is a good method of applying such materials.

One type of anchor is shown in fig. 18. Post support is supplied by the anchor itself. This step-flange anchor is positioned while the concrete is being poured and should be located so that the bottom of the post is about 2 inches above the concrete.

Another type of anchor for solid posts consists of a heavy metal strap shaped in the form of a "U" with or without a bearing plate welded between (fig. 19). These anchors are placed as the concrete pier or slab is being poured. As shown in fig. 18, the post is held in place with bolts.

Fig. 20 illustrates one type of anchor that may be used with double posts. In this and similar cases, the anchor in the concrete is positioned during the pouring operation.

Beam-to-Post Connection

Beams are members to which the floor boards are directly fastened or which support a system of joists. Such beams must be fastened to the supporting posts. Beams may be single large or small members or consist of two smaller members fastened to each side of the posts. When a solid deck is to be constructed, the beams should be sloped at least 1 inch in 8 to 10 feet away from the house.

Single beams when 4 inches or wider usually bear on a post. When this system is used, the posts must be trimmed evenly so that the beam bears on all posts. Use a line level or other method to establish this alignment.

A simple but poor method of fastening a 4- by 4-inch post to a 4- by 8-inch beam, for example, is by toe-nailing (fig. 21A). This is poor practice and should be avoided. Splitting can occur which reduces the strength of the joint. It is also inadequate in resisting twisting of the beam.

A better system is by the use of a 1- by 4-inch lumber or plywood (Exterior grade) cleat located on two sides of the post (fig. 21B). Cleats are nailed to the beam and post with 7d or 8d deformed shank nails.

A good method of post-to-beam connection is by the use of a metal angle at each side (fig. 22A). A 3- by 3-inch angle or larger should be used so that fasteners can be turned in easily. Use lag screws to fasten them in place. A metal strap fastened to the beam and the post might also be used for single beams (fig. 22B). A 1/8- by 3-inch or larger strap, pre-formed to insure a good fit, will provide an adequate connection.

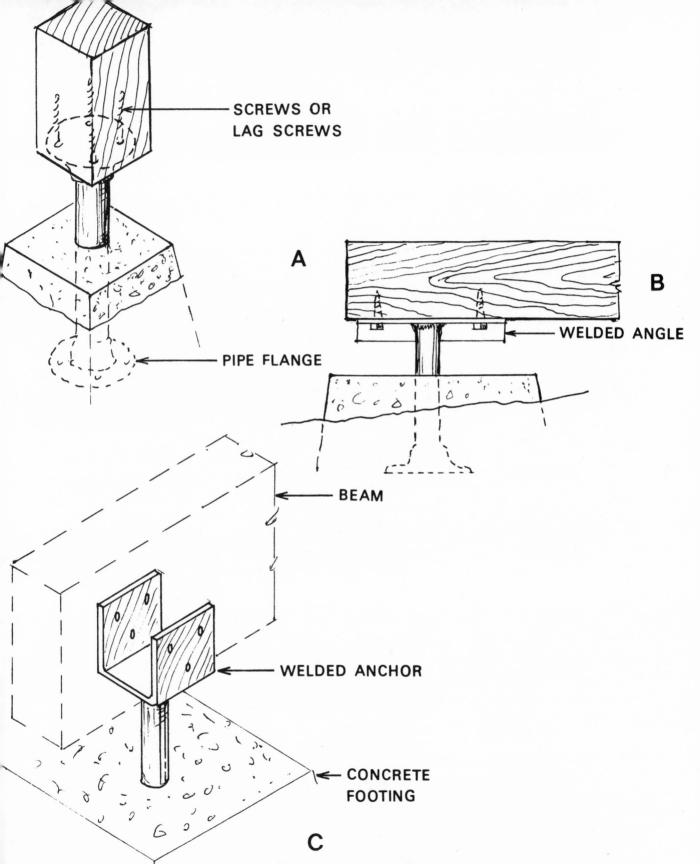

SCREWS OR
LAG SCREWS

A

PIPE FLANGE

B

WELDED ANGLE

BEAM

WELDED ANCHOR

CONCRETE
FOOTING

C

Figure 17. — Pipe and flange anchor. A — pipe flange; B — welded angle (low decks); C — saddle anchor for low decks.

29

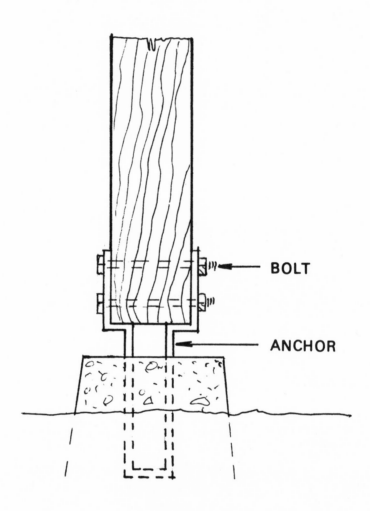

BOLT

ANCHOR

Figure 18. — Step-flange anchor.

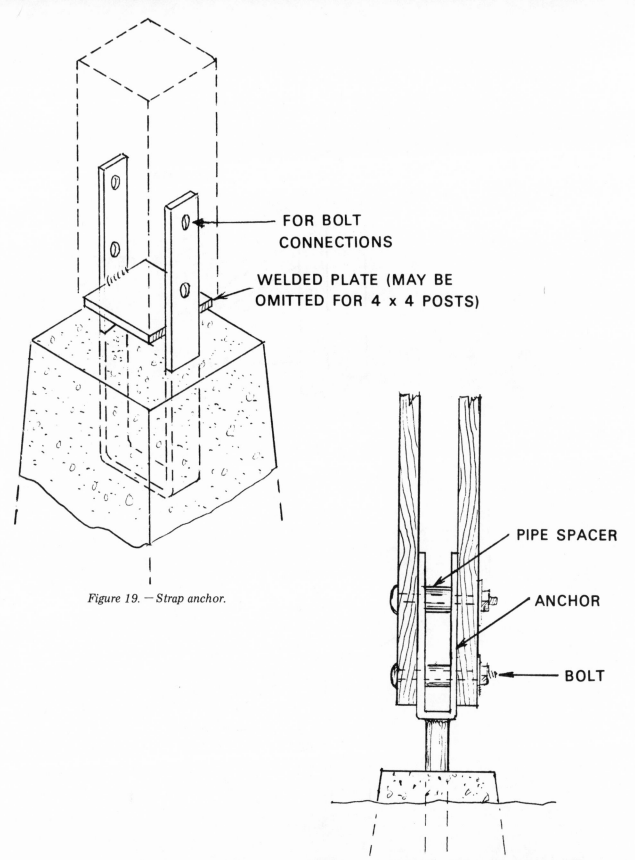

FOR BOLT
CONNECTIONS

WELDED PLATE (MAY BE
OMITTED FOR 4 x 4 POSTS)

Figure 19. — Strap anchor.

PIPE SPACER

ANCHOR

BOLT

Figure 20. — Double post anchor (without bearing plate).

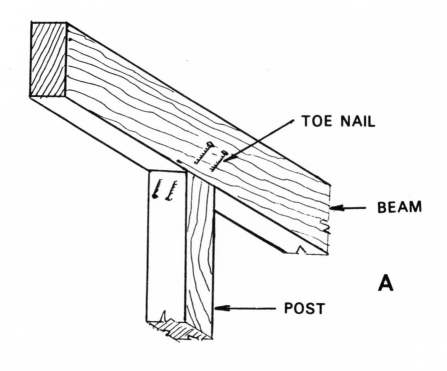

TOE NAIL

BEAM

POST

A

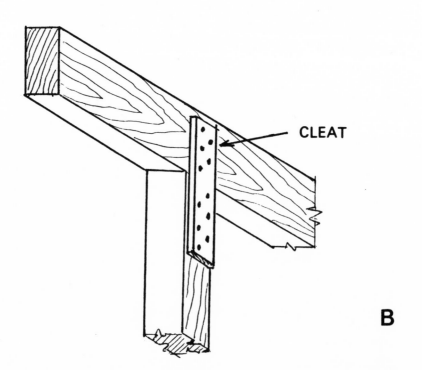

CLEAT

B

Figure 21.—Beam-to-post connection. A—toe-nailing, a poor practice; B—better practice is to use cleat.

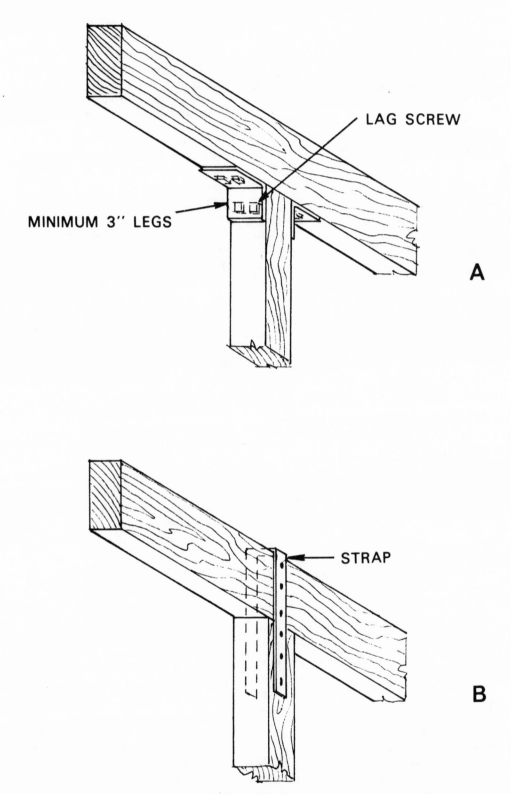

LAG SCREW

MINIMUM 3" LEGS

A

STRAP

B

Figure 22. — Beam-to-post connection. Both A, angle iron, and B, strapping, are good methods.

Use 10^d deformed shank nails for the smaller members and 1/4-inch lag screws for larger members.

A good method of connection for smaller posts and beams consists of a sheet metal flange which is formed to provide fastening surfaces to both beam and post (fig. 23A). The flange is normally fastened with 8^d nails. To prevent splitting, nails should not be located too close to the end of the post. Upper edges of this connector can collect and retain moisture, but this weakness can be minimized somewhat by providing a small groove along the beam for the flange (fig. 23B).

When a **double post** is used, such as two 2-by 6-inch members, a single beam is usually placed between them. One method of terminating the post ends is shown in fig. 24A. This is not fully satisfactory as the end grain of the posts is exposed. Some protection can be had by placing asphalt felt or metal flashing over the joint. Fastening is done with bolts or lag screws. Another method of protection is by the use of cleats over the ends of the posts (fig. 24B).

Double or split beams are normally bolted to the top of the posts, one on each side (fig. 25A). As brought out previously, the load capacity of such a bolted joint depends on the bolt diameter, the number of bolts used, and the resistance of the wood under the bolts. Thus larger diameter bolts should be used to provide greater resistance for the less dense woods (i.e., 1/2-inch rather than 3/8- inch diameter). Notching the top of the beam as shown in fig. 25B provides greater load capacity. A piece of asphalt felt or a metal flashing over the joint will provide some protection for the post end.

Small single beams are occasionally used with larger dimension posts (i.e., 4- by 8-inch beam and 6- by 6-inch post). In such cases, one method of connection consists of bolting the beam directly to the supporting posts (fig. 26A). Some type of flashing should be used over the end of the post.

Another method of connecting smaller beams to larger posts is shown in fig. 26B. A short section of angle iron is used on each side of the post for anchorage and a wood cleat is

then placed to protect the exposed end grain of the larger post.

It is sometimes advantageous to use the post which supports the beam as a railing post. In such a design, the beam is bolted to the post which extends above the deck to support the railing members (fig. 26C).

Beam-and-Joist-to-House Connections

When the deck is adjacent to the house, some method of connecting beams or joists to the house is normally required. This may consist of supporting such members through (a) metal hangers, (b) wood ledgers or angle irons, or (c) utilizing the top of the masonry foundation or basement wall. It is usually good practice to design the deck so that the top of the deck boards are just under the sill of the door leading to the deck. This will provide protection from rains as well as easy access to the deck.

Beams. — One method of connecting the beam to the house consists of the use of metal beam hangers (fig. 27A). These may be fastened directly to a floor framing member such as a joist header or to a 2- by 8-inch or 2- by 10-inch member which has been bolted or lag-screwed to the house framing. Use 6-penny or longer nails or the short, large-diameter nails often furnished with commercial hangers for fastening. Hangers are available for all beams up to 6 by 14 inches in size. In new construction, beam pockets or spaces between floor framing headers can be provided for the deck beam support. Beams can also be secured to the house proper by bearing on ledgers which have been anchored to the floor framing or to the masonry wall with expansion shields and lag screws. The beam should be fastened to the ledger or to the house with a framing anchor or a small metal angle (fig. 27B).

Joists. — When joists of the deck are perpendicular to the side or end of the house, they are connected in much the same manner as beams except that fasteners are smaller. The use of a ledger lag-screwed to the house is shown in fig. 28A. Joists are toe-nailed to the ledger and the house (header or stringer joists) or fastened with small metal clips.

Joists can also be fastened by a 2- by 8-inch or 2- by 10-inch member (lag-screwed to the

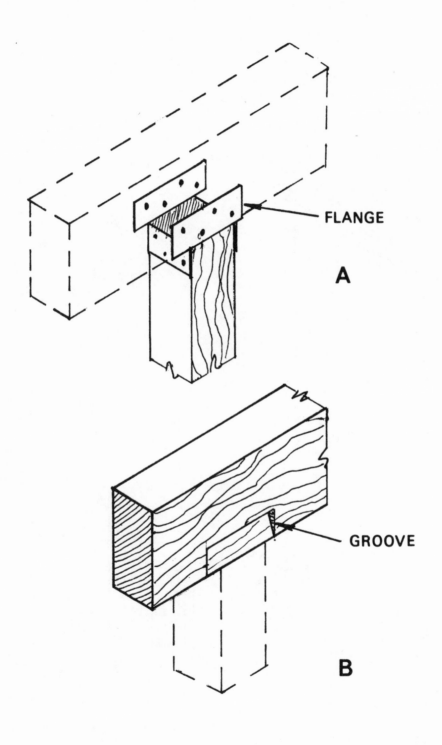

FLANGE

A

GROOVE

B

Figure 23. — Metal flange. A — flange in place; B — groove in beam.

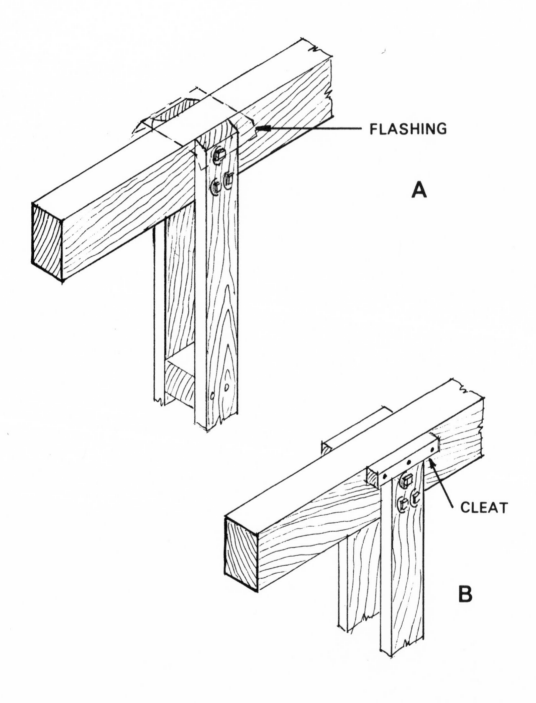

FLASHING

A

CLEAT

B

Figure 24. — Double post to beam. A — post connection with flashing; B — post connection with cleat.

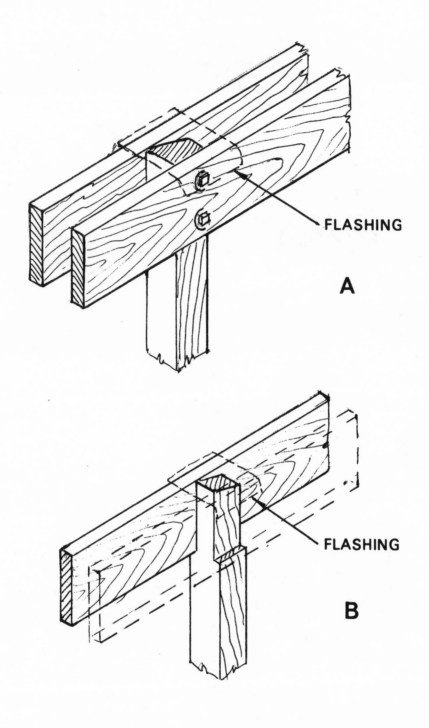

FLASHING

A

FLASHING

B

Figure 25. — Double beam to post. A — bolted joint with flashing; B — notched and bolted joint with flashing.

37

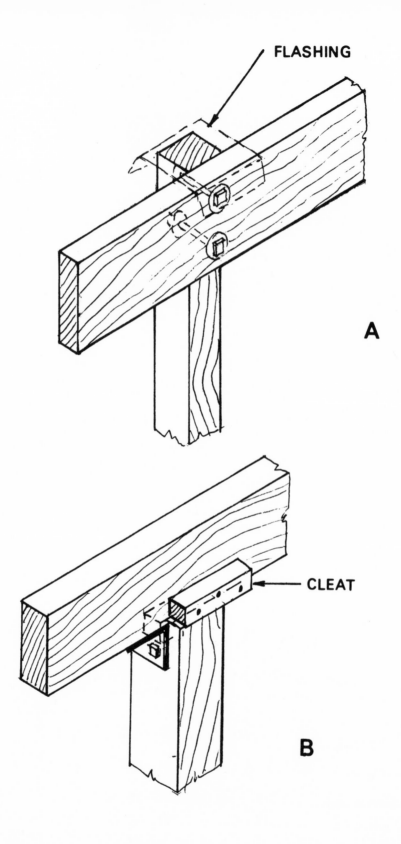

FLASHING

A

CLEAT

B

Figure 26. — Small beam to post. A — bolted connection; B — good connection for large post; C — extension of post for rail.

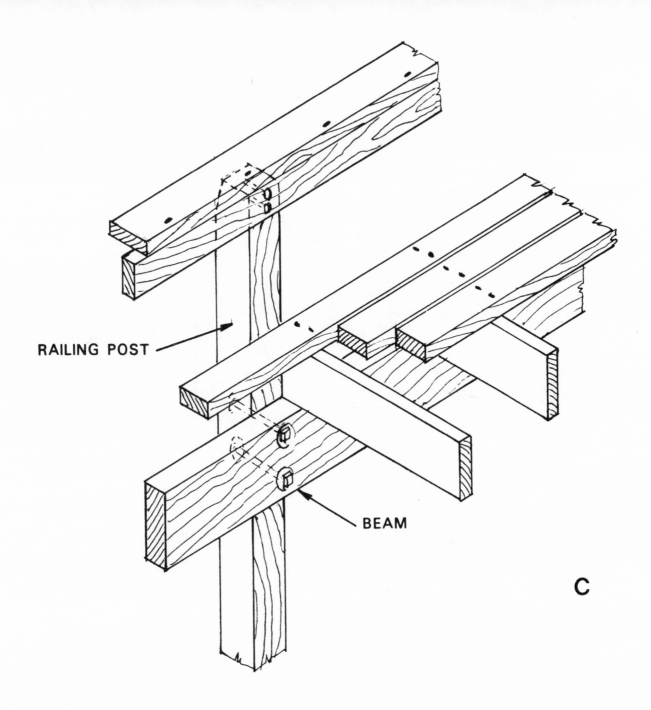

RAILING POST

BEAM

C

house) by means of joist hangers (fig. 28B). Six-penny nails or 1-1/4-inch galvanized roofing nails are used to fasten the hangers to the joist and to the header. When joists or beams are parallel to the house, no ledger or other fastening member is normally required (fig. 28C). If they are supported by beams, the beams, of course, are then connected to the house, as previously illustrated.

Bracing

On uneven sites or sloping lots, posts are often 5 or more feet in height. When the deck is free (not attached to the house), it is good practice to use bracing between posts to provide lateral resistance. Treated poles or posts embedded in the soil or in concrete footings usually have sufficient resistance to lateral forces,

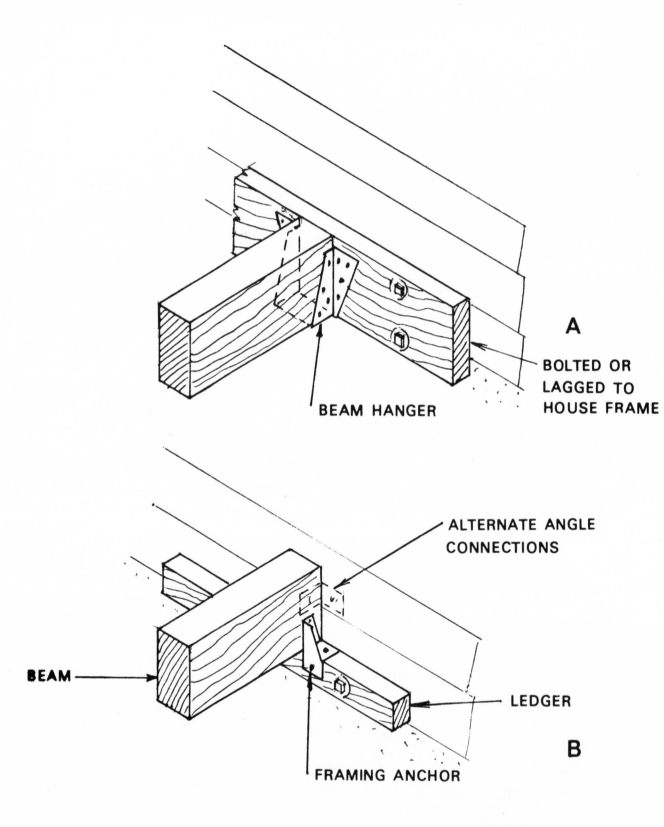

A

BOLTED OR
LAGGED TO
HOUSE FRAME

BEAM HANGER

ALTERNATE ANGLE
CONNECTIONS

BEAM

LEDGER

B

FRAMING ANCHOR

Figure 27. — Beam to house. A — beam hanger; B — ledger support.

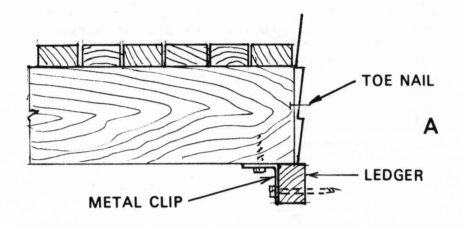

TOE NAIL

A

LEDGER

METAL CLIP

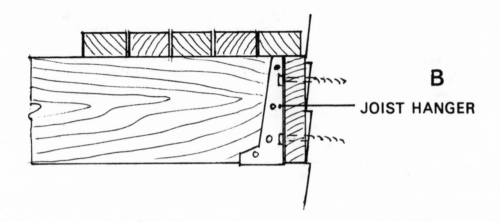

B

JOIST HANGER

SUPPORTING MEMBER
FASTENED TO HOUSE

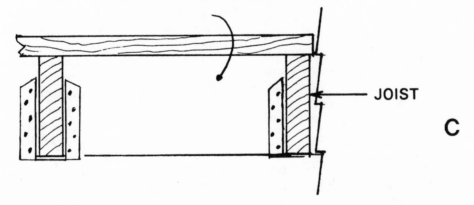

JOIST

C

Figure 28. — Joist to house. A — ledger support; B — joist hangers; C — unconnected joists.

and such construction normally requires no additional bracing. However, when posts rest directly on concrete footings or pedestals, and unsupported heights are more than about 5 feet, some system of bracing should be used. Braces between adjacent posts serve the same purpose as bracing in the walls of a house.

Special bracing in the horizontal plane is normally not needed for residential decks of moderate area and height. Decks can be braced efficiently in the horizontal plane by installing galvanized steel strap diagonals just under the deck surface. These should be in pairs in the direction of both diagonals and securely fastened at both ends. An alternative is to use flat 2- by 4-inch or 2- by 6-inch members across one diagonal, securely nailed to the underside of the deck members. In the case of a very large, high deck, it is advisable to consult a design engineer for an adequate bracing procedure.

Types of bracing. — Bracing should be used on each side of a "free" deck to provide racking resistance in each direction. Single bracing (one member per bay) should consist of 2-inch dimension material. When brace length is no greater than 8 feet, 2- by 4-inch members can be used; 2- by 6-inch braces should be used when lengths are over 8 feet. Fastenings should normally consist of lag screws or bolts (with washers) to fasten 2-inch braces to the posts. See section, "Fasteners," for proper fastener use.

One simple system of single bracing is known as the "W" brace which can be arranged as shown in fig. 29A. Braces are lag-screwed to the post and joined along the centerline. When desired and when space is available, braces can be placed on the inside of the posts.

Another single bracing method between posts is shown in fig. 29B. Braces are located from the base of one post to the top of the adjacent posts. Braces on the adjacent side of the deck should be placed in the opposite direction.

Another system of bracing used between posts is the "X" or cross brace (fig. 29C). When spans and heights of posts are quite great, a cross brace can be used at each bay. However, bracing at alternate bays is normally sufficient. A bolt may be used where the 2-inch braces cross to further stabilize the bay. One-inch

thick lumber bracing is not recommended as it is subject to mechanical damage such as splitting at the nails.

When posts are about 14 feet or more in height, which could occur on very steep slopes, two braces might be required to avoid the use of too long a brace. Such bracing can be arranged as shown in fig. 29D.

Partial bracing. — A plywood gusset brace, or one made of short lengths of nominal 2-inch lumber, can sometimes be used as a partial brace for moderate post heights of 5 to 7 feet. A plywood gusset on each side of a post can also serve as a means of connection between a post and beam (fig. 30A). Use 3/4-inch exterior-type plywood and fasten to the post and beam with two rows of 10^d nails. The top edge of the gusset should be protected by an edge or header member which extends over the plywood.

A partial brace made of 2- by 4-inch lumber can be secured to the beam and posts with lag screws or bolts as shown in fig. 30B. Some member of the deck, such as the deck boards or a parallel edge member, can overlap the upper ends to protect the end grain from moisture. When an overlap member is not available and the area is sufficient for two fasteners, a vertical cut can be used for the brace.

Fastening braces. — Brace-to-post connections should be made to minimize trapped moisture or exposed end grain yet provide good resistance to any racking stresses. The detail in fig. 31A has exposed end grain and should be avoided unless protected by an overlapping header or other member above. Fig. 31B shows a more acceptable cut. No end grain of the brace is exposed. Use two lag screws (or bolts) for 2- by 4-inch and 2- by 6-inch braces.

When two braces join at a post, such as occurs in a "W" brace, connection should be made on the centerline as shown in fig. 32A. A tight joint provides the resistance of all fasteners when one brace is in compression, but there is some hazard in trapped moisture. Fig. 32B shows a spaced joint which is preferred when constant exposure to moisture is a factor.

A flush brace may be used if desired from the standpoint of appearance (fig. 33). This type connection requires that a backing cleat be lagged or bolted to each side of the post. The braces are then fastened to the cleats as shown.

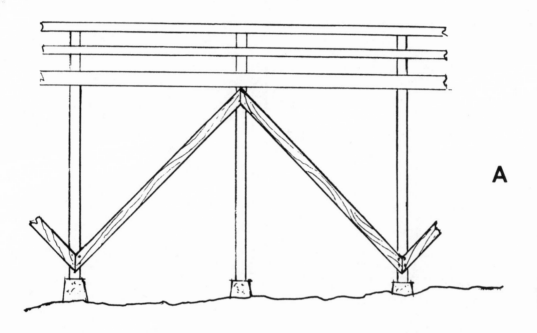

A

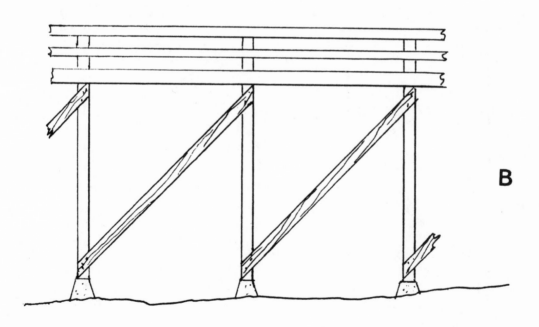

B

Figure 29. — Bracing. A — "W" brace; B — single direction brace.

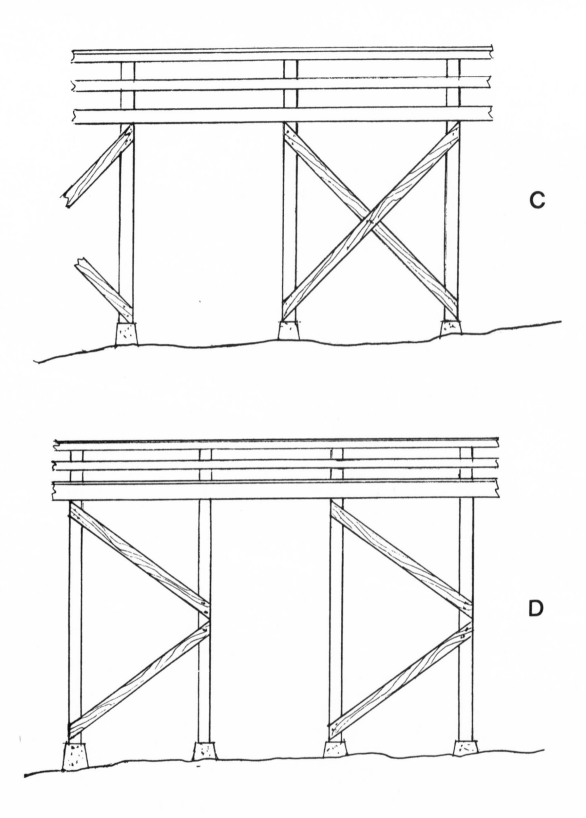

Figure 29. — Bracing (continued). C — cross brace; D — bracing for high posts.

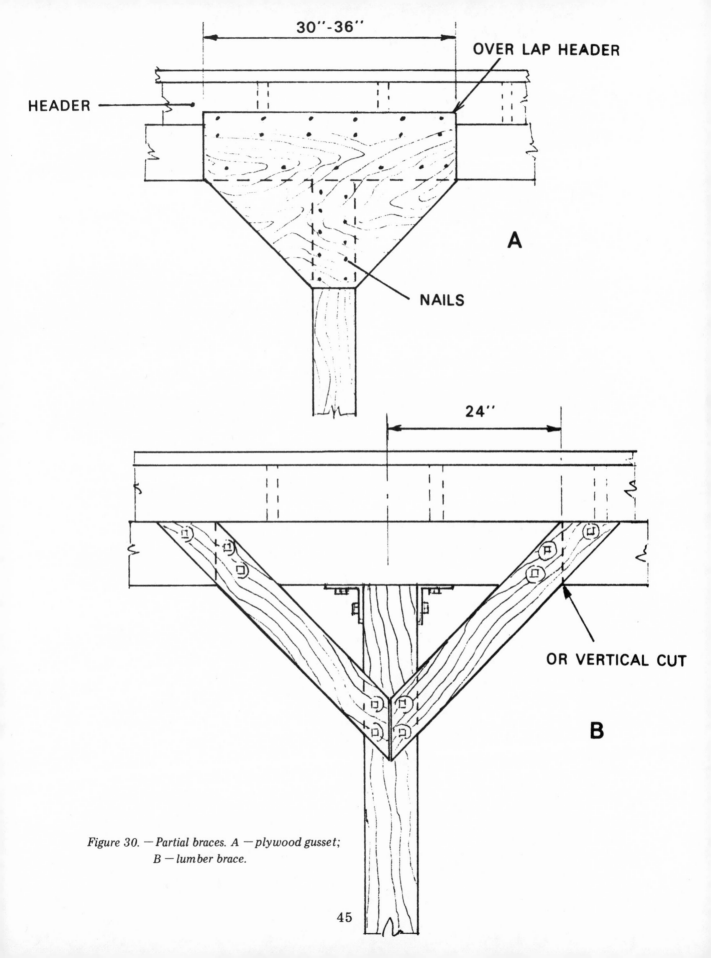

30"-36"

OVER LAP HEADER

HEADER

NAILS

A

24"

OR VERTICAL CUT

B

Figure 30. — Partial braces. A — plywood gusset;
B — lumber brace.

45

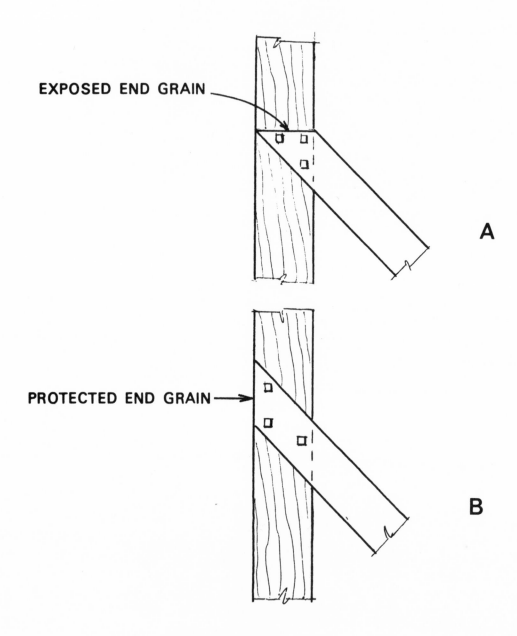

EXPOSED END GRAIN

A

PROTECTED END GRAIN →

B

Figure 31. — Brace cuts. A — poor practice; B — better practice.

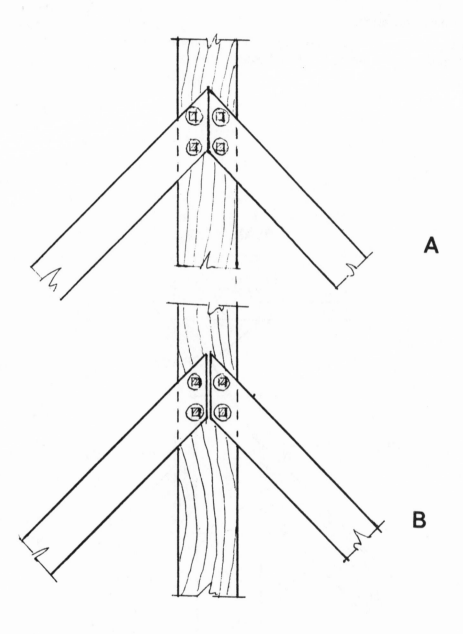

Figure 32. — Joint at post. A — tight joint; B — open joint (preferred).

The use of large, galvanized washers or other means of isolating the brace from the post will provide a smaller area for trapping moisture behind the brace (fig. 34). Such a spacer at each bolt or lag screw might be used when the less decay-resistant wood species are involved.

Joist-to-Beam Connections

When beams are spaced 2 to 5 feet apart and 2- by 4-inch Douglas-fir or similar deck boards are used, there is no need to use joists to support the decking. The beams thus serve as both fastening and support members for the 2-inch deck boards. However, if the spans between beams are more than 3-1/2 to 5 feet apart, it is necessary to use joists between the beams or 2 by 3 or 2 by 4 on edge for decking (see table 4). To provide rigidity to the structure, the joists must be fastened to the beam in one of several ways.

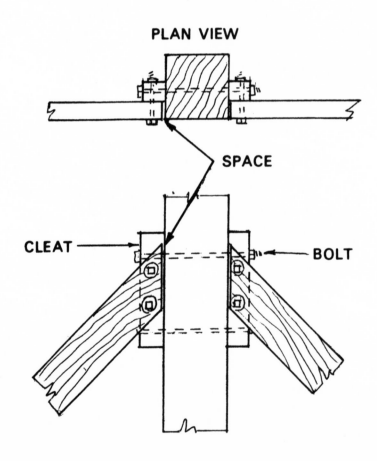

PLAN VIEW

SPACE

CLEAT

BOLT

Figure 33. — Flush brace.

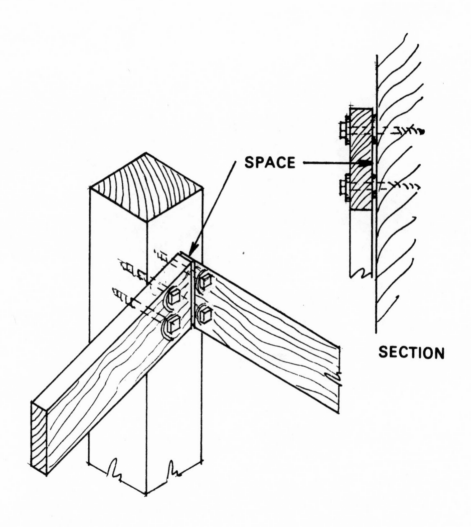

SPACE

SECTION

Figure 34. — Spaced brace.

Joists bearing directly on the beams may be toe-nailed to the beam with one or two nails on each side (fig. 35A). Use 10^d nails and avoid splitting. When uplift stresses are inclined to be great in high wind areas, supplementary metal strapping might be used in addition to the toe-nailing (fig. 35B). Use 24- to 26-ga. galvanized strapping and nail with 1-inch galvanized roofing nails. When a header is used at the joist ends, nail the header into the end of each joist (fig.

35C). Have the header overhang the beam by one-half inch to provide a good drip edge.

Joists located between beams and flush with their tops may be connected in two manners. One utilizes a 2- by 3-inch or 2- by 4-inch ledger which is spiked to the beam. Joists are cut between beams and toe-nailed to the beams at each end (fig. 36A). The joint can be improved by the use of small metal clips.

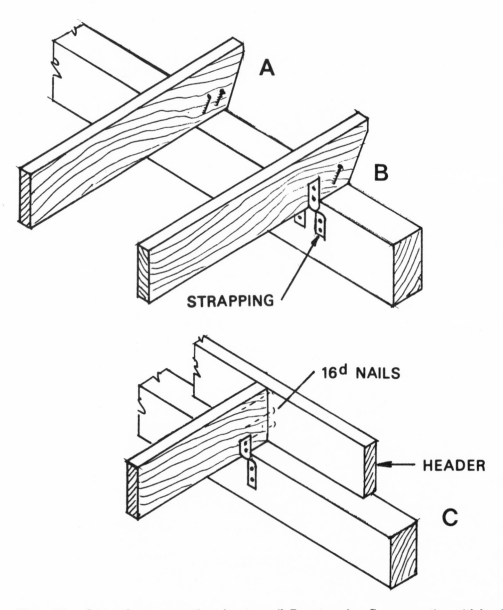

A

B

STRAPPING

16^d NAILS

HEADER

C

Figure 35. — Joist-to-beam connection. A — toe nail; B — strapping; C — connection with header.

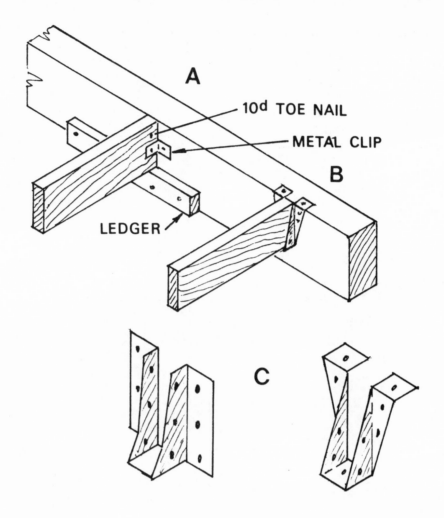

Figure 36. — Joists between beams. A — ledger support; B — joist hanger support; C — joist hangers.

Another method utilizes a metal joist hanger (fig. 36B). The hanger is first nailed to the end of the joist with 1- to 1-1/4-inch galvanized roofing nails and then to the beam. Several types of joist hangers are available (fig. 36C).

Fastening Deck Boards

Deck boards are fastened to floor joists or to beams through their face with nails or screws. Screws are more costly to use than nails from the standpoint of material and labor but have greater resistance to loosening or withdrawal than the nail. A good compromise between the common smooth shank nail and the screw is the deformed shank nail (see "Fasteners"). These

nails retain their withdrawal resistance even under repeated wetting and drying cycles. Both nails and screws should be set flush or just below the surface of the deck board.

Some good rules in fastening deck boards to the joists or beams are as follows:

1. Number of fasteners per deck board — use two fasteners for nominal 2- by 3-inch and 2- by 4-inch decking laid flat (fig. 37A). For 2 by 3's or 2 by 4's on edge, use one fastener per joist (fig. 37B).
2. Size of fasteners —
   Nails (deformed shank, galvanized, aluminum, etc.):

   Nominal 2-inch thick deck boards — 12d

51

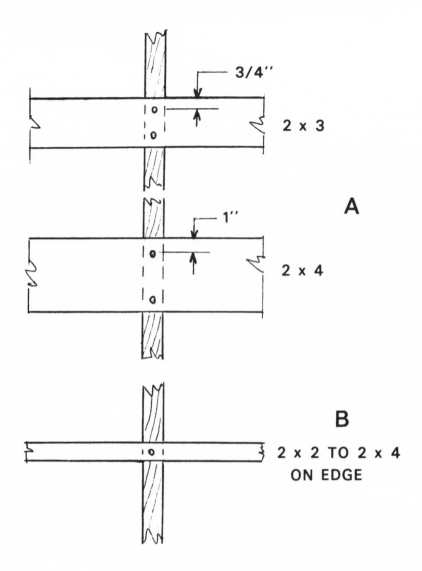

Figure 37. — Fastening deck boards. A — flat deck boards; B — deck boards on edge.

Nominal 2- by 3-inch deck boards on edge — 5 inch

Nominal 2- by 4-inch deck board (nailing not recommended)

Screws (flat or oval head, rust proof):

Nominal 2-inch thick deck boards — 3 inch

Nominal 2- by 3-inch deck boards on edge — 4-1/2 inch

Nominal 2- by 4-inch deck boards on edge — 5 inch.

3. Spacing — space all deck boards (flat or vertical) one-eighth to one-fourth inch apart (use 8^d or 10^d nail for 1/8-inch spacing).

4. End joints (butt joints) — end joints of flat deck boards should be made over the center of the joist or beam (fig. 38A). In flat grain boards, always place with the bark side up (fig. 38B). When the upper face gets wet, it crowns slightly and water drains off more easily. End joints of any deck boards on edge should be made over a spaced double joist (fig. 39A), a 4-inch or wider single beam, or a nominal 2-inch joist with nailing cleats on each side (fig. 39B).

When deck boards are used on edge, spacers between runs will aid in maintaining uniform spacing and can be made to effect lateral support between runs by using lateral nailing at the spacers. Spacers as shown in fig. 39C are recommended between supports when spans exceed 4 feet and should be placed so that no distance between supports or spacers exceeds 4 feet. An elastomeric construction adhesive or penta-grease on both faces of each spacer prevents water retention in the joints.

Always dip ends of deck boards in water-repellent preservative before installing.

Always pre-drill ends of 2- by 3-inch or 2- by 4-inch (flat) deck boards of the denser species, or when there is a tendency to split. Pre-drill when screws are used for fastening. Pre-drill all fastening points of 2- by 3-inch or 2- by 4-inch deck boards placed on edge.

To provide longer useful life for decks made of low to moderate decay-resistant species, use one or more of the following precautions:
(1) Use spaced double joists or beams and place end joints between (fig. 40).
(2) Lay a strip of building felt saturated with a wood preservative over the beam or joist before installing deck boards.
(3) Apply an elastomeric glue to the beam or joist edge before installing the deck boards.
(4) Treat end joints of deck boards made over a support with yearly applications of a water-repellent preservative. (A plunger-type oil can will work well.)

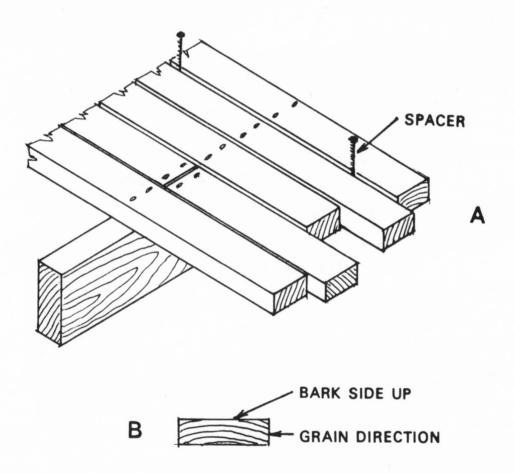

Figure 38. — Fastening flat deck boards. A — spacing between boards; B — grain orientation for flat grain boards.

Fastening Plywood

Plywood panels should generally be installed with a minimum 1/16-inch space between edge and end joints, using the support spacing and nailing schedule indicated in table 6. When caulking is used, a joint space of at least one-fourth inch is usually required.

To avoid unnecessary moisture absorption by the plywood, seal all panel edges with an exterior primer or an aluminum paint formulated for wood. The panel edge sealant can be most conveniently applied prior to installation, while the plywood is still in stacks. Build some slope into the deck area to provide for adequate drainage. A minimum slope of 1 inch in 8 to 10 feet should be provided when installing the joists or beams.

Provide ventilation for the underside of the deck areas in all cases. For low-level decks, this can be done by leaving the space between the joists open at the ends and by excavating material away from the support joists and beams. For high-level decks over enclosed areas, holes can be drilled in the blocking between joists.

Railing Posts

Low-level decks located just above the grade normally require no railings. However, if the site is sloped, some type of protective railing or

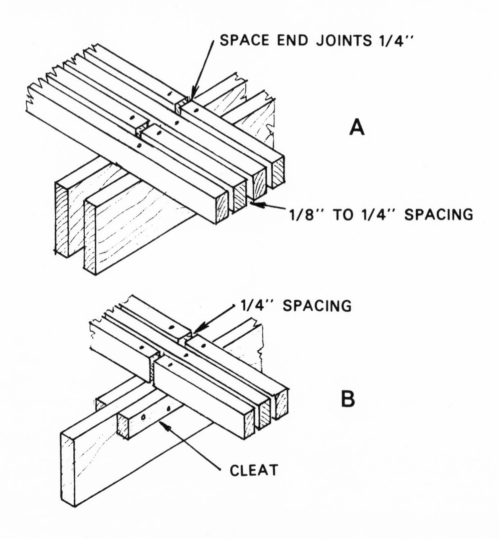

Figure 39. — Fastening "on edge" deck boards. A — installing over double joist or beam; B — installing over single joist or beam; C — spacers for 2x4 decking on edge.

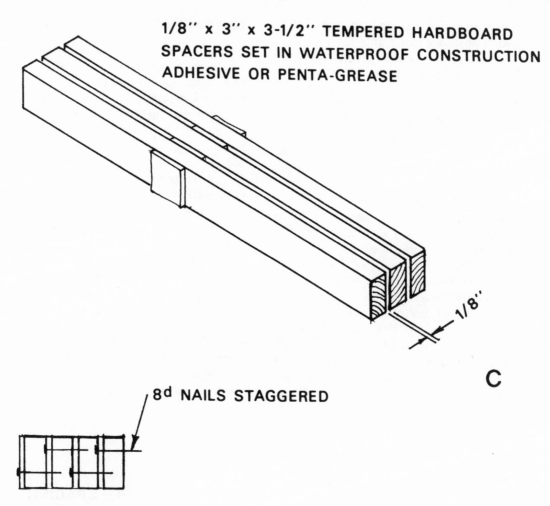

1/8" x 3" x 3-1/2" TEMPERED HARDBOARD SPACERS SET IN WATERPROOF CONSTRUCTION ADHESIVE OR PENTA-GREASE

1/8"

C

8ᵈ NAILS STAGGERED

SECTION SHOWING NAILING

system of balusters might be needed, because of the height of the deck.

The key members of a railing are the posts. Posts must be large enough and well fastened to provide strength to the railing. Some type of vertical member such as the post can also serve as a part of a bench or similar edge structure of the deck. Railings should be designed for a lateral load of at least 20 pounds per lineal foot. Thus, posts must be rigid and spaced properly to resist such loads.

One method of providing posts for the deck railing is by the extension of the posts which support the beams (fig. 41). When single or double beams are fastened in this manner, the posts can extend above the deck floor and serve for fastening the railing and other horizontal members. Railing heights may vary between 30 and 40 inches, or higher when a bench or wind screen is involved. Posts should be spaced no more than 6 feet apart for a 2 by 4 horizontal top rail and 8 feet apart when a 2 by 6 or larger rail is used.

When supporting posts cannot be extended above the deck, a joist or beam may be available to which the posts can be secured. Posts can then be arranged as shown in fig. 42A. Such posts can be made from 2 by 6's for spans less than 4 feet, from 4 by 4's or 2 by 8's for 4- to 6-foot spans, and from 4 by 6's or 3 by 8's for 6- to 8-foot spans. Each post should be bolted to the edge beam with two 3/8-inch or larger bolts determined by the size of the post. This system can also be used when the railing consists of a number of small baluster-type posts (fig. 42B). When such posts are made of 2- by 2- or 2- by 3-inch members and spaced 12 to 16 inches apart, the top fastener into the beam should be a 1/4- or 3/8-inch bolt or lag screw. The bottom fastener can then be a 12^d or larger deformed shank nail. Pre-drill when necessary to prevent splitting. Wider spacings or larger size posts require two bolts. A 1/8-inch to 1/4-inch space should be allowed between the ends of floor boards and posts.

The ends of beams or joists along the edge of the deck can also be used to fasten the railing posts. One such fastening system is shown in fig. 43. Single or double (one on each side) posts are bolted to the ends of the joists or beams. Space the bolts as far apart as practical for better lateral resistance.

The practice of mounting posts on a deck board should be avoided. Not only is the railing structurally weak, but the bottom of the post has end grain contact with a flat surface. This could induce high moisture content and possible decay.

Deck Benches

High-deck benches. — At times there is an advantage in using a bench along the edge of a high deck, combining utility with protection. One such design is shown in fig. 44. The vertical back supporting members (bench posts), spaced no more than 6 feet apart, are bolted to the beams. They can also be fastened to extensions of the floor joists. When beams are more than 6 feet apart, the bench post can be fastened to an edge joist in much the same manner as railing posts. The backs and seat supports should be spaced no more than 6 feet apart when nominal 2-inch plank seats are used.

Low-deck benches. — Benches can also be used along the edge of low decks. These can be simple plank seats which serve as a back drop for the deck. Such bench seats require vertical members fastened to the joists or beams with cross cleats (fig. 45). For nominal 2-inch plank seats, vertical supports should be bolted to a joist or beam and be spaced no more than 6 feet apart. A single wide support (2 by 10) (fig.

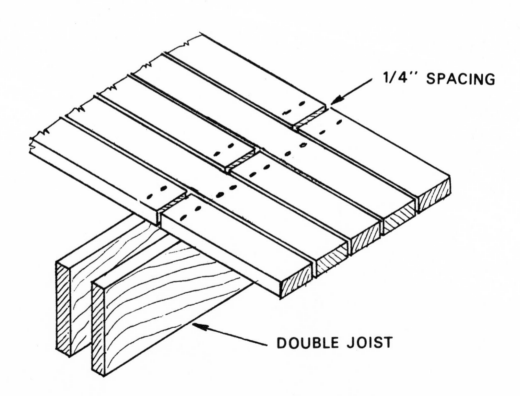

Figure 40. — End joints of decking over double joist.

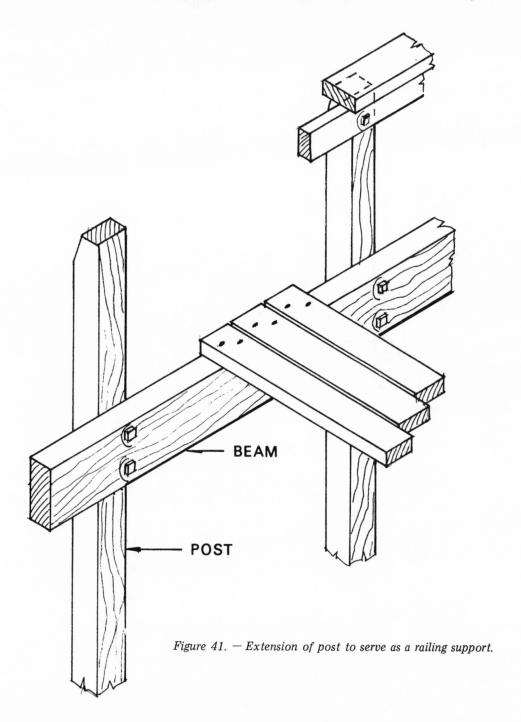

BEAM

POST

Figure 41. — Extension of post to serve as a railing support.

45A) or double (two 2 by 4's) supports (fig. 45B) can be used. Cleats should be at least 2 by 3 inches in size.

Such member arrangements can also be used as a step between two decks with elevation differences of 12 to 16 inches. Many other bench arrangements are possible; but spans, fastenings, and elimination of end grain exposure should always be considered.

Railings

Horizontal railings. — The top horizontal members of a railing should be arranged to protect the end grain of vertical members such as posts or balusters. A poorly designed railing detail is shown in fig. 46. Such details should be avoided, as the end grain of the baluster-type posts is exposed. Fig. 47 is an improvement,

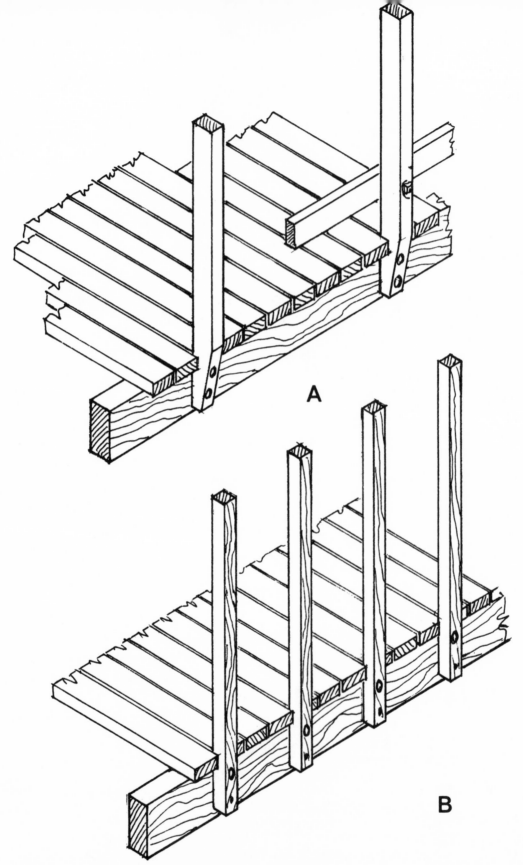

Figure 42. — Railing posts fastened to edge of deck member. A — spaced posts (4 feet and over); B — baluster-type posts.

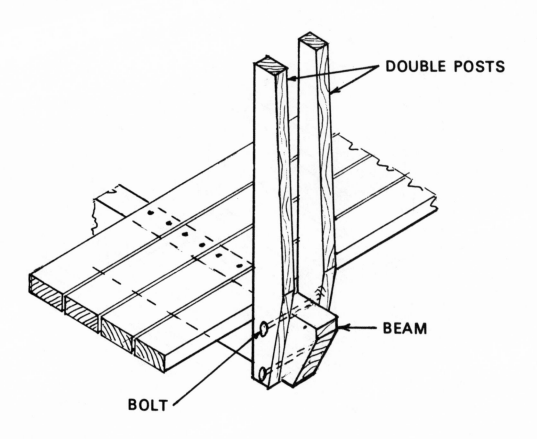

Figure 43. — Double railing posts at beam or joist ends.

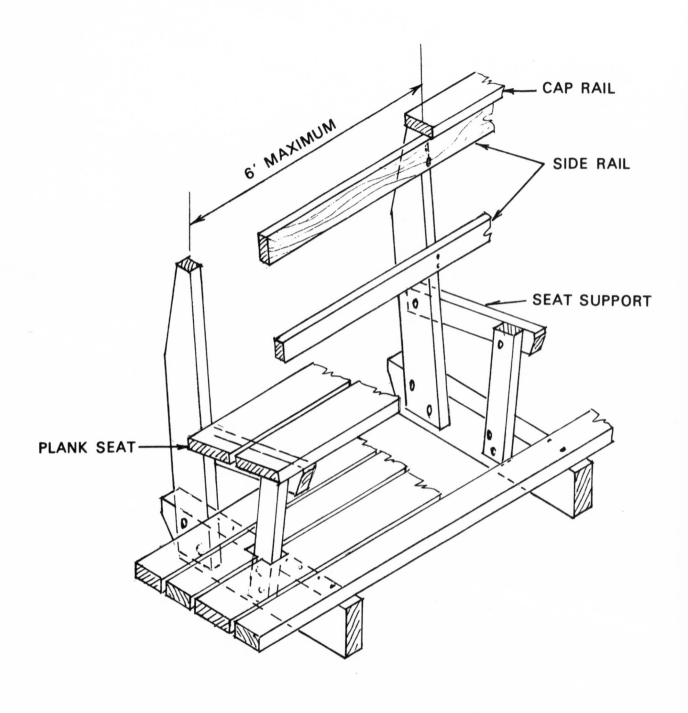

CAP RAIL

SIDE RAIL

SEAT SUPPORT

6' MAXIMUM

PLANK SEAT

Figure 44. — Deck bench.

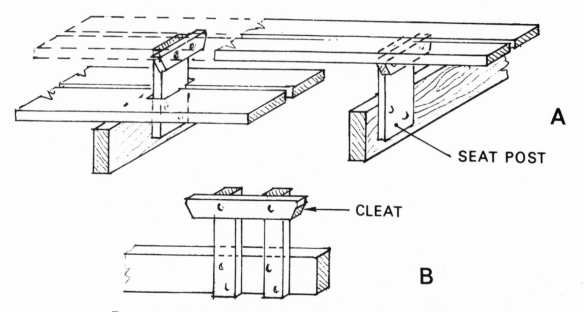

A

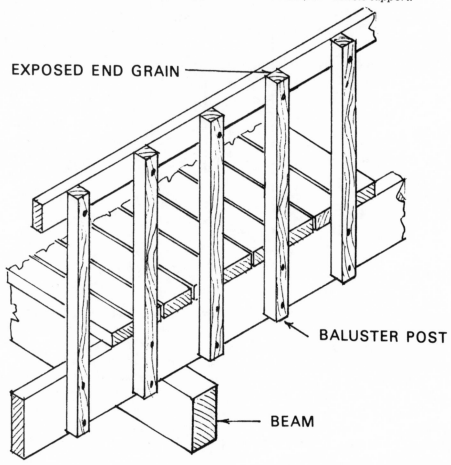

Figure 45. — Bench seats. A — single support and cross cleat; B — double support.

SEAT POST

CLEAT

B

EXPOSED END GRAIN

BALUSTER POST

BEAM

Figure 46. — Poorly designed railing detail.

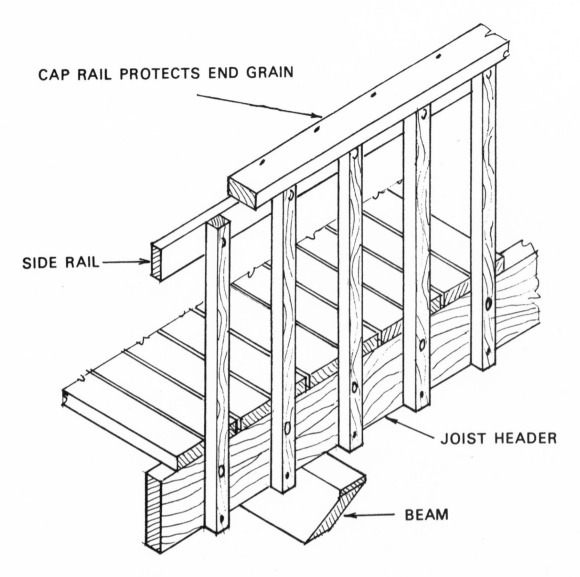

CAP RAIL PROTECTS END GRAIN

SIDE RAIL

JOIST HEADER

BEAM

Figure 47. — Good railing detail.

as the end grain of the balusters is protected by the cap rail.

The upper side rail, which is usually a 2- by 4-inch or wider member, should be fastened to the posts with a lag screw or bolt at each crossing. The cap rail then can be nailed to the edge of the top rail with 12^d deformed shank nails spaced 12 to 16 inches apart.

When railing posts are spaced more than about 2 feet apart, additional horizontal members may be required as a protective barrier (fig. 48). These side rails should be nominal 2- by 4-inch members when posts are spaced no more

than 4 feet apart. Use 2 by 6's when posts are spaced over 4 feet apart.

Rail fastenings. — When the upper side rail is bolted to the post (fig. 48), the remaining rails can be nailed to the posts. Use two 12^d deformed shank nails at each post and splice side rails and all horizontal members at the centerline of a post. Posts must be more than 2 inches in thickness to provide an adequate fastening area at each side of the center splice.

A superior rail termination consists of the use of a double post (fig. 49). Horizontal members are spaced about 1 inch apart, which al-

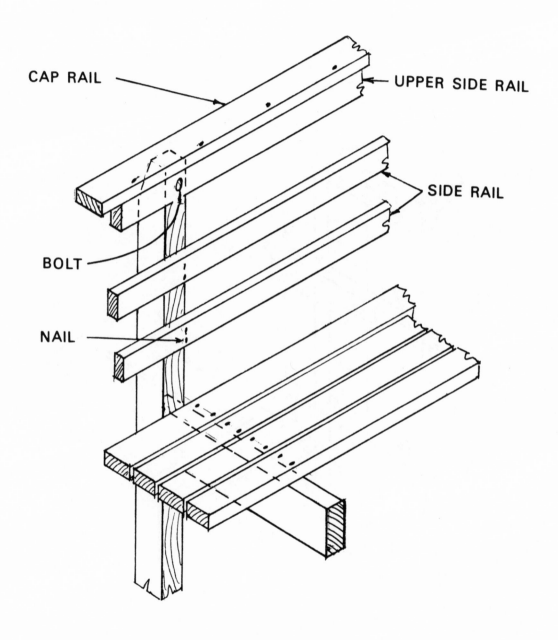

CAP RAIL

UPPER SIDE RAIL

SIDE RAIL

BOLT

NAIL

Figure 48. — Side rails for deck railing.

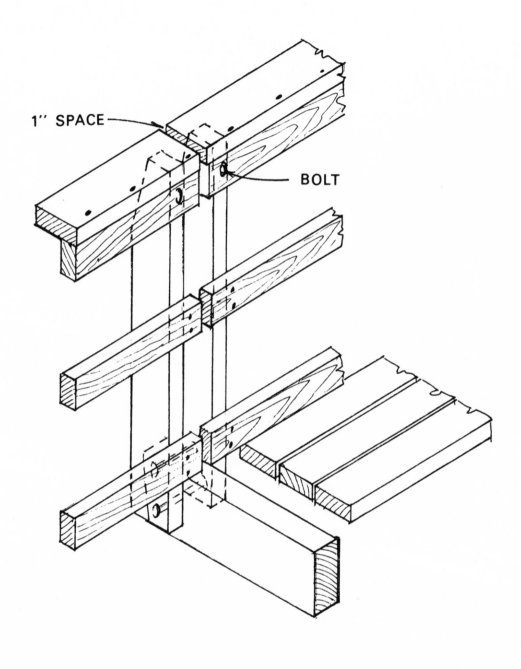

1" SPACE

BOLT

Figure 49. — Spaced rail joints — good practice.

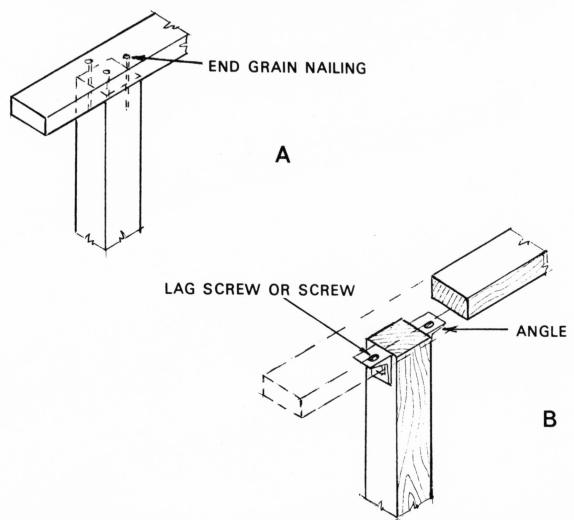

Figure 50. — Fastening cap rail to post. A — nailed (end grain), a poor practice; B — angle iron connection, a good practice.

lows ends of members to dry quickly after rains. As in all wood deck members, the ends should always be dipped in water-repellent preservative before assembly.

Cap rail connections. — A good method of fastening cap rail to the post has been shown in the previous section and in fig. 47. In some designs, however, the cap rail without additional members may be specified. An unsatisfactory method of connecting a cap rail to the post is by nailing (fig. 50A). End grain nailing is not recommended in such connections. A better method is shown in fig. 50B. Short lengths of galvanized angle irons are fastened to the post with lag screws or bolts. The cap rail is then fastened with short (1-1/2 - inch) lag

screws. Although this is certainly not as simple as nailing, it provides an excellent joint and fastenings are not exposed to the weather.

Miscellaneous rail connections. — There may be occasions in the construction of a railing of a deck to use members between the posts rather than lapping the posts. This might be in construction of an adjoining wind screen or mid-height railings between posts. Such connections might also be adaptable to fences where horizontal members are located between posts. The connection to the post is the important one, as it must be rigid as well as minimize areas where moisture could be trapped. Dado cuts for a 2-inch rail are shown in figs. 51A and 51B. Although these are reasonably good struc-

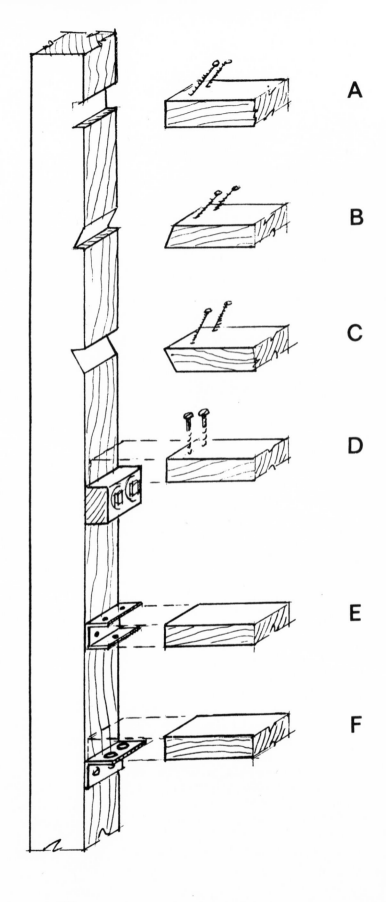

Figure 51. — Rail-to-post connections.
A-C — dado cuts (not recommended);
D — wood block support;
E — metal connector;
F — angle iron.

turally, moisture could be retained at the end grain of the bottom cut. Fig. 51C shows the notch reversed. This will not retain moisture as much as the previous cuts, but the member must be cut precisely to provide a rigid joint. A wood block lag screwed to the side of the post serves as a good fastening area for the rail (fig. 51D). This is a good connection when the rail is spaced slightly away from the post. The rail should be fastened to the block with screws.

A commercial-type bracket is shown in fig. 51E. This connector can also be used to advantage for 1-inch members used in a fence or a wind screen. Another good method utilizes a small angle iron lagged to the post (fig. 51F). The rail is then fastened to the angle with lag screws from below.

Stairways

There is often a need for a stairway as an access to a deck or for use between decks with different levels. Exterior stairs are much the same as stairs within a house, except that details which avoid trapped moisture or exposed end grain of the members should be used.

Research has indicated that for woods with moderate to low decay resistance, a three-minute dip in a water repellent preservative for all members at least tripled the average service life of exterior stairways and their parts (12). Use of all-heartwood of decay-resistant species or of pressure-treated wood will insure even longer life.

Stair stringers. — A basic stair consists of stair stringer (sometimes called stair carriage) and treads. Additional parts include balusters and side cap rails and, on occasion, risers. The supporting members of a stair are the stringers. Stringers are used in pairs spaced no more than 3 feet apart. They are usually made of 2- by 10-inch or 2- by 12-inch members. Stringers must be well secured to the framing of the deck. They are normally supported by a ledger or by the extension of a joist or beam. A 2- by 3-inch or 2- by 4-inch ledger nailed to the bottom of an edge framing member with 12^d nails supports the notched stringer (fig. 52A). Toe-nailing or small metal clips are used to secure the carriage in place. Stair stringers can also be bolted to the ends of joists or beams when they are spaced no more than about 3 feet apart (fig.

52B). Use at least two 1/2-inch galvanized bolts to fasten the stringer to the beam or joist.

The bottom of the stair stringers should be anchored to a solid base and be isolated from any moisture source. Two systems frequently used consist of metal angles anchored to a concrete base (figs. 53A and 53B). The angles should be thick enough to raise the stringer off the concrete, which should also be sloped for drainage. They might also be fastened to a treated wood member anchored in the concrete or in the ground.

Tread and riser size. — The relation of the tread width ("run") to the riser height is important in determining the number of steps required. For ease of ascent, the rise of each step in inches times the width of the tread in inches should equal 72 to 75 (fig. 54A). Thus, if the riser is 8 inches (considered maximum for stairs), the tread would be 9 inches. Or if the riser is 7-1/2 inches, the tread should be about 10 inches. Thus, the number of risers and treads can be found when the total height of the stair is known. Divide total rise in inches by 7-1/2 (each riser) and select the nearest whole number. Thus, if the total rise is 100 inches, the number of risers would be 13 and the total run, about 120 inches (fig. 54B).

Tread support. — Stair treads can be supported by dadoes cut into the stringer (fig. 55A). Stringers can also be notched to form supports for the tread and riser (fig. 55B). However, both methods introduce end grain exposure and possible trapped moisture and should be avoided for exposed stairs, especially when untreated, low decay-resistant species are used.

A better method of tread support consists of 2- by 4-inch ledgers or cleats bolted to the stair stringers and extended to form supports for the plank treads (fig. 56A). The ledgers can be sloped back slightly so that rain will drain off the treads. Ledgers might also be beveled slightly to minimize tread contact. Nail 2- by 10-inch or 2- by 12-inch treads to the ledgers with three 12^d deformed shank nails at each stringer. Rust-proof wood screws 3 inches in length can also be used. Always place plank treads with bark side up to prevent cupping and retention of rain water. Treads can also be made of two 2- by 6-inch planks, but the span must be limited to 42 inches for the less-dense woods (fig. 56B).

Another method of fastening the stair cleats

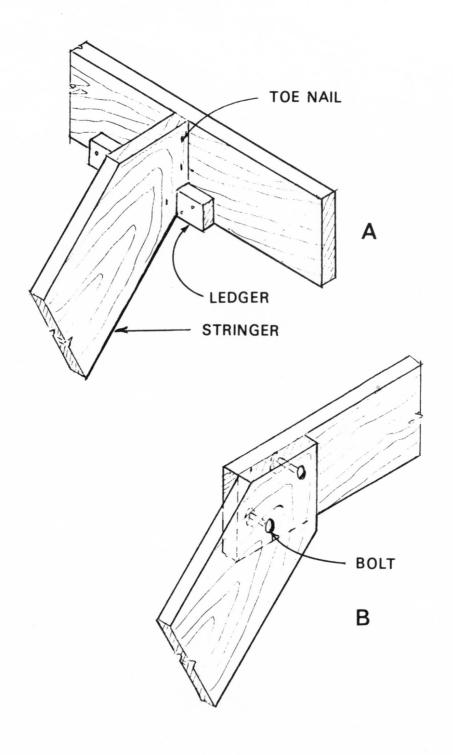

TOE NAIL

LEDGER

STRINGER

A

BOLT

B

Figure 52. — Stair stringer supports. A — ledger; B — bolt.

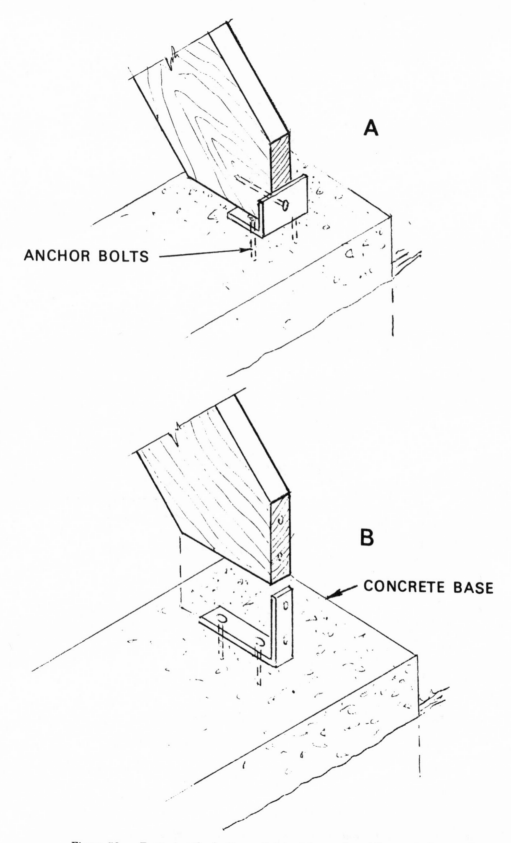

ANCHOR BOLTS

A

B

CONCRETE BASE

Figure 53. — Fastening the bottom of stair stringer. A and B — angle iron anchors.

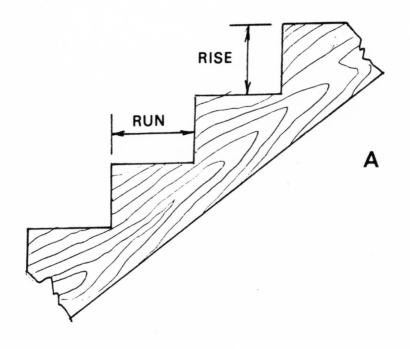

RISE

RUN

A

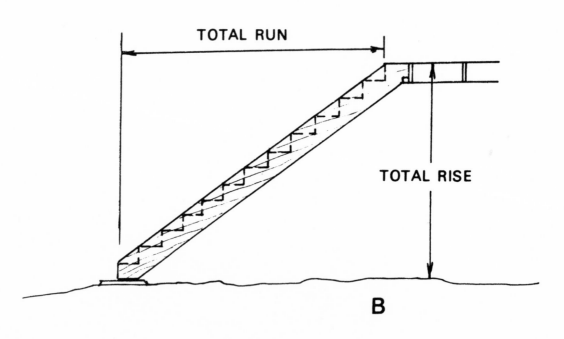

TOTAL RUN

TOTAL RISE

B

Figure 54. — Riser-to-tread relationship. A — individual step. B — total rise and run.

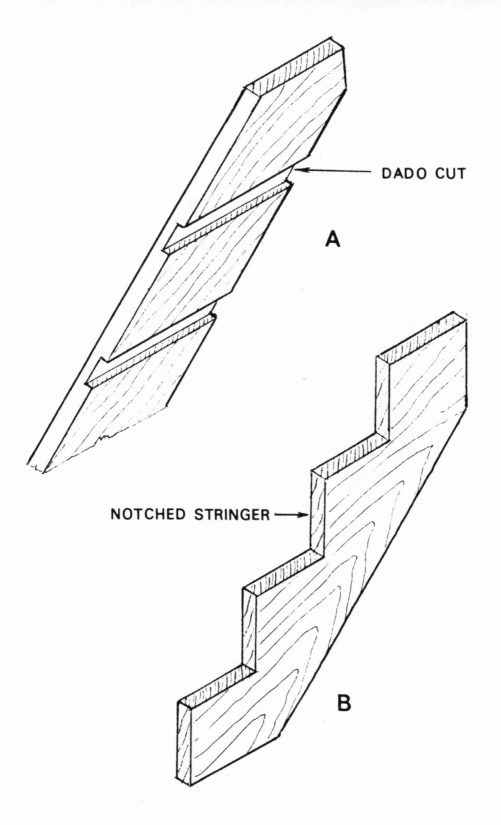

DADO CUT

A

NOTCHED STRINGER

B

Figure 55. — Tread supports (not recommended). A — dadoed stringer (poor practice); B — notched (better practice).

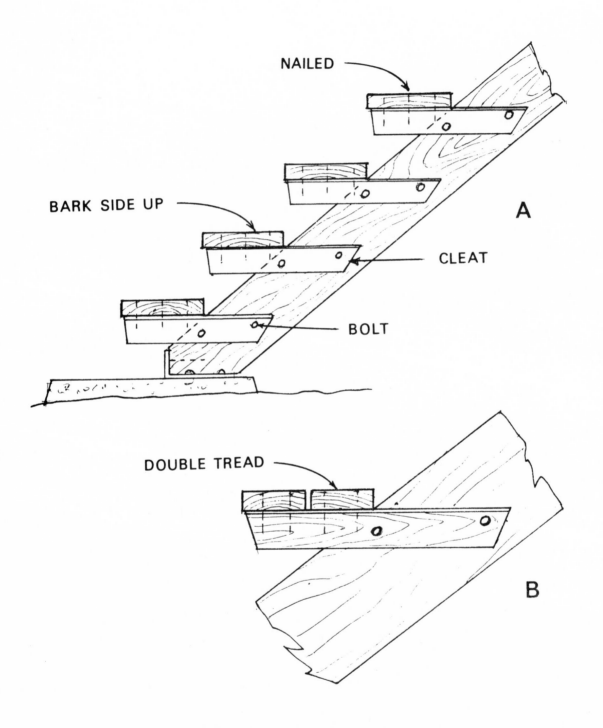

NAILED

BARK SIDE UP

CLEAT

BOLT

A

DOUBLE TREAD

B

Figure 56. — Stairways with cleat support. A — extended cleat with single tread (good practice); B — double tread (better practice); C — nailed cleat (poor practice).

is by nailing them directly to the stair stringers (fig. 56C). Use 2- by 3-inch or 2-by 4-inch cleats and fasten with three or four 12^d deformed shank nails. Treads are then nailed to the cleats in a normal manner. This method is not as resistant to exposure as the extended cleat shown in fig. 56A, because there are more areas for trapped moisture. However, with the use of a decay-resistant species and water-repellent preservative treatment, good service should result.

Stair railings. — On moderate to full height stairs with one or both sides unprotected, some type of railing is advisable. Railings for stairs are constructed much the same as railings for the deck. In fact, from the standpoint of appearance, they should have the same design. Railings normally consist of posts fastened to stair stringers and supplementary members such as top and intermediate rails.

One method similar to a deck rail uses widely spaced posts and protective railings (fig. 57). Posts are 2- by 4-inch members when spacing is no more than 3 feet and 3- by 4-inch or 2- by 6-inch members for spacings from 3 to 6 feet. Longitudinal cap rails, top and intermediate, are normally 2- by 4-inch or wider members. Assembly should be with bolts or lag screws. The cap rail can be nailed to the top rail with 12^d deformed shank nails spaced 12 to 16 inches apart.

The design shown in fig. 58 has closely spaced posts which serve as balusters. Each should be bolted to the stringer and to a top rail. The cap rail which also protects the baluster ends can then be nailed to the adjoining rail.

A single cap railing can also be used for such stairs, but it is advisable to fasten it to the posts with metal clips or angles to eliminate unreliable end-grain fastening.

Many other variations of post and rail combination can be used. All designs should consider safety and utility as well as a pleasing appearance. A well-designed deck, railing, and stairway combination with care in details will provide years of pleasure with little maintenance.

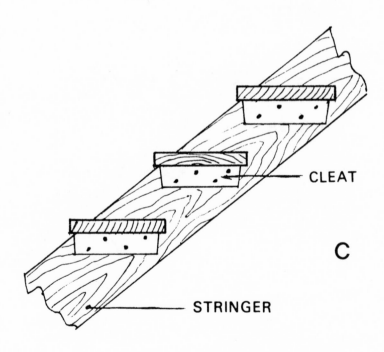

CLEAT

C

STRINGER

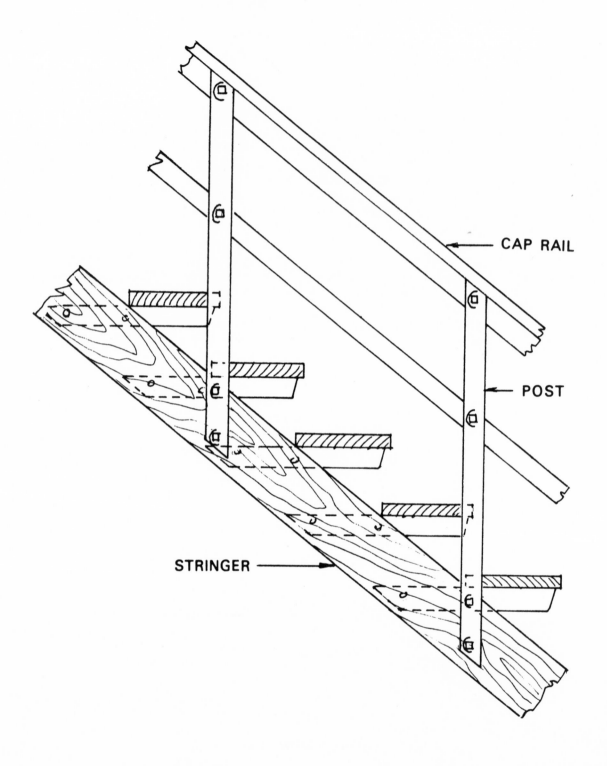

CAP RAIL

POST

STRINGER

Figure 57. — Widely spaced stair posts.

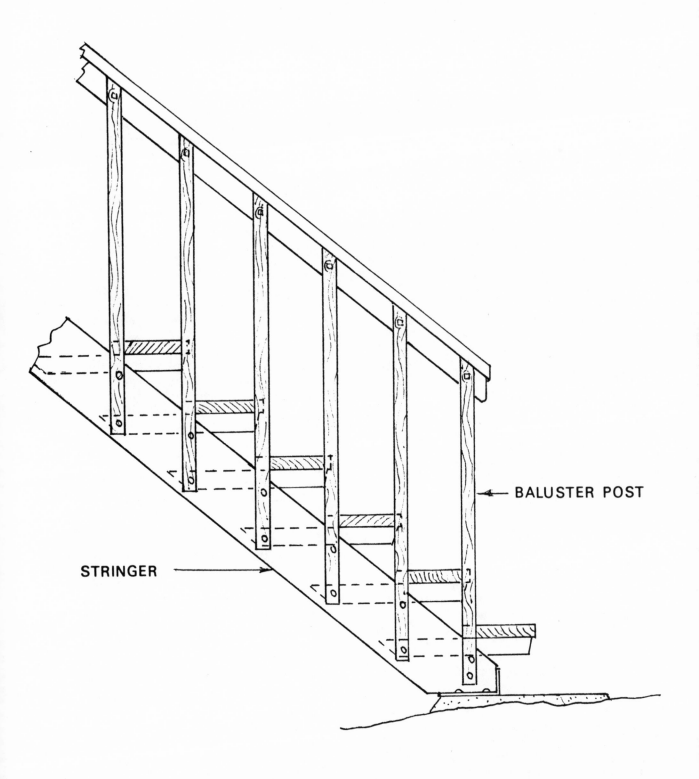

BALUSTER POST

STRINGER

Figure 58. — Baluster-type stair posts.

WOOD PRESERVATION

(Abridged from Chapter 18, Wood Handbook.)

Wood can be protected from the attack of decay fungi, harmful insects, or marine borers by applying selected chemicals as wood preservatives. The degree of protection obtained depends on the kind of preservative used and on achieving proper penetration and retention of the chemicals. Some preservatives are more effective than others, and some are more adaptable to certain use requirements. The wood can be well protected only when the preservative substantially penetrates it, and some methods of treatment assure better penetration than others. There is also a difference in the treatability of various species of wood, particularly of their heartwood, which generally resists preservative treatment more than sapwood.

Good wood preservatives, applied with standard retentions and with the wood satisfactorily penetrated, substantially increase the life of wood structures, often by five or more times. On this basis the annual cost of treated wood in service is greatly reduced below that of similar wood without treatment. In considering preservative treatment processes and wood species, the combination must provide the required protection for the conditions of exposure and life of the structure.

WOOD PRESERVATIVES

Wood preservatives fall into two general classes: Oils, such as creosote and petroleum solutions of pentachlorophenol; and waterborne salts that are applied as water solutions.

Preservative Oils

The wood does not swell from the preservative oils, but it may shrink if it loses moisture during the treating process. Creosote and solutions with the heavier, less volatile petroleum oils often help protect the wood from weathering outdoors, but may adversely influence its cleanliness, odor, color, paintability, and fire resistance in use. Preservative oils sometimes travel from treated studs or subflooring along nails and discolor adjacent plaster or finish flooring. Volatile oils or solvents with oil-borne preservatives, if removed after treatment, leave the wood somewhat cleaner than the heavier oils but may not provide as much protection. Wood treated with preservative oils can be glued satisfactorily, although special processing or cleaning may be required to remove surplus oils from surfaces before spreading the adhesive.

Coal-Tar Creosote

Coal-tar creosote, a black or brownish oil made by distilling coal tar, is one of the more important and useful wood preservatives. Its advantages are: (1) High toxicity to wood-destroying organisms; (2) relative insolubility in water and low volatility, which impart to it a great degree of permanence under the most varied use conditions; (3) ease of application; (4) ease with which its depth of penetration can be determined; (5) general availability and relative low cost (when purchased in wholesale quantities); and (6) long record of satisfactory use.

The character of the tar used, the method of distillation, and the temperature range in which the creosote fraction is collected all influence the composition of the creosote. The composition of the various coal-tar creosotes available, therefore, may vary to a considerable extent. Small differences in composition, however, do not prevent creosotes from giving good service; satisfactory results in preventing decay may generally be expected from any coal-tar creosote that complies with the requirements of standard specifications.

Although coal-tar creosote or creosote-coal tar solutions are well qualified for general outdoor service in structural timbers, they have properties that are disadvantageous for some purposes.

The color of creosote and the fact that creosote-treated wood usually cannot be painted satisfactorily make this preservative unsuitable for finish lumber or other lumber used where appearance and paintability are important.

The odor of creosoted wood is unpleasant to some persons. Also, creosote vapors are harmful to growing plants, and foodstuffs that are sensitive to odors should not be stored where creosote odors are present. Workmen sometimes object to creosoted wood because it soils their clothes and because it burns the skin of the face and hands of some individuals. With normal precautions to avoid direct dermal contact with creosote, there appears to be no danger to the health of workmen handling or working near the treated wood or on the health of the occupants of buildings in which the treated wood is used.

Freshly creosoted timber can be ignited easily and will burn readily, producing a dense smoke. However, after the timber has seasoned some months, the more volatile parts of the oil disappear from near the surface, and the creosoted wood usually is little, if any, easier to ignite than untreated wood. Until this volatile oil has evaporated, ordinary precautions should be taken to prevent fires. On the other hand, timber that has been kept sound by creosote treatment is harder to ignite than untreated wood that has started to decay. A preservative other than creosote should be used where fire hazard is highly important, unless the treated wood is also protected from fire.

A number of specifications prepared by different organizations are available for creosote oils of different kinds. Although the oil obtained under most of these specifications will probably be effective in preventing decay, the requirements of some organizations are more exacting than others. Federal Specification TT–C–645 for coal-tar creosote, adopted for use by the U.S. Government, will generally prove satisfactory; under normal conditions, this specification can be met without difficulty by most creosote producers. The requirements of this specification are similar to those of the American Wood-Preservers' Association (AWPA) Standard P1 for creosote, which is equally acceptable.

Federal Specification TT–C–645 provides for three classes of coal-tar creosote. Class I is for poles; class II is for ties, lumber, structural timbers, land or fresh water piles, and posts; and class III is for piles, lumber, and structural timbers for use in coastal waters.

Some pole users, to reduce bleeding in poles with high retentions of creosote, have specified lower retentions of coal-tar creosote fortified with 2 percent pentachlorophenol. Corrosion problems to treating plant equipment have accompanied the use of this preservative and are under investigation.

Coal-Tar Creosotes for Nonpressure Treatments

Special coal-tar creosotes are available for nonpressure treatments. They differ somewhat from regular commercial coal-tar creosote in (1) being crystal-free to flow freely at ordinary temperatures and (2) having low-boiling distillation fractions removed to reduce evaporation in thermal (hot-and-cold) treatments in open tanks. Federal Specification TT–C–655 covers coal-tar creosote for brush, spray, or open-tank treatments.

Other Creosotes

Creosotes distilled from tars other than coal tar are used to some extent for wood preservation, although they are not included in current Federal or AWPA specifications. These include wood-tar creosote, oil-tar creosote, and water-gas-tar creosote. These creosotes protect wood from decay and insect attack but are generally less effective than coal-tar creosote.

Tars

Coal tars are seldom used alone for preserving wood because good penetration is usually difficult to obtain and because they are less poisonous to wood-destroying fungi than the coal-tar creosotes. Service tests have demonstrated that surface coatings of tar are of little value. Coal tar has been used in the pressure treatment of crossties, but it has been difficult to get the highly viscous tar to penetrate wood satisfactorily. When good absorptions and deep penetrations are obtained, however, it is reasonable to expect a satisfactory degree of effectiveness from treatment with coal tar. The tar has been particularly effective in reducing checking in crossties in service.

Water-gas-tar is used less extensively than coal tar, but, in certain cases where the wood was thoroughly impregnated, the results were good.

Creosote Solution

For many years, either coal tar or petroleum oil has been mixed with coal-tar creosote, in various proportions, to lower preservative costs. These creosote solutions have a satisfactory record of performance, particularly for crossties where they have been most commonly used.

Federal Specification TT–C–650, "Creosote-Coal-Tar Solution," covers five classes of creosote-coal-tar solution. These classes contain not less than 80, 70, 60, 50, and 65 percent coal-tar distillate (creosote) (by volume), for classes I, II, III, IV, and V, respectively. Classes I and II are for land and fresh-water piles, posts, lumber, structural timber, and bridge ties. Classes III and IV are for crossties and switch ties. Class V, which has a 60 to 75 percent level of distillate, is for piles, lumber, and structural timber used in coastal waters.

AWPA Standard P2 includes four creosote-coal-tar solutions that must contain, respectively, not less than 80, 70, 60, or 50 percent by volume of coal-tar distillate and must also meet requirements as to physical and chemical properties. AWPA Standard P12 covers a creosote-coal-tar solution for the treatment of marine (coastal waters) piles and timbers. Federal Specification TT–W–568 and AWPA Standard P3 stipulate that creosote-petroleum oil solutions shall contain not less than 50 percent (by volume) of coal-tar creosote and the petroleum oil shall meet the requirements of AWPA's Standard P4.

Creosote-coal-tar solutions, compared to straight creosote, tend to reduce weathering and checking of the treated wood. The solutions may have a greater tendency to accumulate on the surface of the treated wood (bleed) and may penetrate the wood with greater difficulty, particularly because they generally are more viscous than straight creosote. Higher temperatures and pressures during treatment, when they can safely be used, will often improve penetration of solutions of high viscosity.

Even though petroleum oil and coal tar are less toxic to wood-destroying organisms than straight creosote, and their mixtures with creosote are also less toxic in laboratory tests, a reduction in toxicity does not imply less preservative protection. Creosote-petroleum solutions and creosote coal-tar solutions help to reduce checking and weathering of the treated wood. Frequently posts and ties treated with these solutions of standard formulation have shown better service than those similarly treated with straight coal-tar creosote.

Pentachlorophenol Solutions

Water-repellent solutions containing chlorinated phenols, principally pentachlorophenol, in solvents of the mineral spirits type, were first used in commercial treatments of wood by the millwork industry about 1931. Commercial pressure treatment with pentachlorophenol in heavy petroleum oils started on poles about 1941, and considerable quantities of various products were soon pressure treated. AWPA Standard P8 and Federal Specification TT–W–570 define the properties of pentachlorophenol and AWPA Standard P9 covers solvents for oil-borne preservatives. A commercial process using pentachlorophenol dissolved in liquid petroleum gas was introduced in 1961.

Pentachlorophenol solutions for wood preservation generally contain 5 percent (by weight) of this chemical although solutions with volatile solvents may contain lower or higher concentrations. The performance of pentachlorophenol and the properties of the treated wood are influenced by the properties of the solvent used. The heavy petroleum solvent included in AWPA Standard P9A is preferable for maximum protection, particularly where the wood treated with pentachlorophenol is used in contact with the ground, but further evaluation of newer volatile solvents is needed.

The heavy oils remain in the wood for a long time and do not usually provide a clean or paintable surface. The volatile solvents, such as liquefied petroleum gas and methylene chloride, are used with pentachlorophenol when the natural appearance of the wood must be retained and the treated wood requires a paint coating or other finish. Because of the toxicity of pentachlorophenol, care is necessary to avoid excessive personal contact with the solution or vapor in handling and using it.

A "bloom" preventive, such as ester gum or oil-soluble glycol, is generally required with volatile solvents to prevent crystals of pentachlorophenol from forming on the surface of the treated wood. Brushing or washing the surface with hot water or an alkaline solution has been used to remove the crystalline deposits.

The results of pole service and field tests on wood treated with 5 percent pentachlorophenol in a heavy petroleum oil are similar to those with coal-tar creosote. This similarity has been recognized in the preservative retention requirements of treatment specifications. Pentachlorophenol is ineffective against marine borers and is not recommended for the treatment of marine piling or timbers used in coastal waters.

Water-Repellent Preservatives

Preservative systems containing water-repellent components are sold under various trade names, principally for the dip or equivalent treatment of window sash and other millwork. Federal Specification TT–W–572 stipulates that such preservatives consist of volatile solvents, such as mineral spirits, that do not cause appreciable swelling of the wood, and that the treated wood be paintable and meet a performance test on water repellency. In pressure treatment with water-repellent preservative, however, considerable difficulty has been experienced in removing residual solvents and obtaining acceptable paintability.

The preservative chemicals in Federal Specification TT–W–572 may be not less than 5 percent of pentachlorophenol, not less than either 1 or 2 percent (for tropical conditions) of copper in the form of copper naphthenate, or not less than 0.045 percent copper in the form of copper-8-quinolinolate (for uses where foodstuffs will be in contact with the treated wood). Commercial Standard CS 262–63, covering the water-repellent preservative, non-pressure treatment for millwork, permits other preservatives provided their toxicity properties are as high as those of 5 percent (by weight) pentachlorophenol solution. Mixtures of other chlorinated phenols with pentachlorophenol meet this requirement according to tests by the National Woodwork Manufacturer's Association.

Water-repellent preservative containing copper-8-quinolinolate has been used in non-pressure treatment of wood containers, pallets, and other products for use in contact with foods. That preservative is also included in AWPA Standard P8. Here it is intended for use in volatile solvents to pressure-treat lumber for decking of trucks and cars or for related uses involving harvesting, storage, and transportation of foods.

Effective water-repellent preservatives will retard the ingress of water when wood is exposed above ground. They therefore help reduce dimensional changes in the wood due to moisture changes when the wood is exposed to rainwater or dampness for short periods. As with any wood preservative, their effectiveness in protecting wood against decay and insects depends upon the retention and penetration obtained in application.

Waterborne Preservatives

Standard wood preservatives used in water solution include acid copper chromate, ammoniacal copper arsenite, chromated copper arsenate (types I, II, and III), chromated zinc chloride, and fluor chrome arsenate phenol. These preservatives are often employed when cleanliness and paintability of the treated wood are required. The chromated zinc chloride and fluor chrome arsenate phenol formulations resist leaching less than preservative oils, and are seldom used where a high degree of protection is required for wood in ground contact or for other wet installations. Several formulations involving combinations of copper, chromium, and arsenic have shown high resistance to leaching and very good performance in service. The ammoniacal copper arsenite and chromated copper arsenate are now included in specifications for such items as building foundations, building poles, utility poles, marine piling, and piling for land and fresh water use.

Test results based on sea water exposure have shown that dual treatment (waterborne copper-containing salt preservatives followed by coal-tar-creosote) is possibly the most effective method of protecting wood against all types of marine borers. The AWPA standards have recognized this process as well as the treatment of marine piling with high retentions of ammoniacal copper arsenite or chromated copper arsenate. The recommended treatment and retention in pounds per cubic foot (p.c.f.) for round timber piles exposed to severe marine borer hazard are:

	Southern pine, red pine (P.c.f.)	Coastal Douglas-fir (P.c.f.)	AWPA standard
Severe borer hazard:			
Limnoria tripunctata only:			
Ammoniacal copper arsenite	2.5	2.5	C3 C18
Chromated copper arsenate	2.5	2.5	C3 C18
Limnoria tripunctata and Pholads (dual treatment):			
First treatment:			
Ammoniacal copper arsenite	1.0	1.0	C3 C18
Chromated copper arsenate	1.0	1.0	C3 C18
Second treatment:			
Creosote	20.0	20.0	C3 C18
Creosote-coal-tar	20.0	Not recommended	C3 C18

Waterborne preservatives leave the wood surface comparatively clean, paintable, and free from objectionable odor. With several exceptions, they must be used at low treating temperatures (100° to 150° F.) because they are unstable at the higher temperatures. This may involve some difficulty when higher temperatures are needed to obtain good treating results in such woods as Douglas-fir. Because water is added during treatment, the wood must be dried afterward to the moisture content required for use.

Waterborne preservatives, in the retentions normally specified for wood preservation, decrease the danger of ignition and rapid spread of flame, although formulations with copper and chromium stimulate and prolong glowing combustion in carbonized wood.

Acid Copper Chromate

Acid copper chromate (Celcure) contains, according to Federal Specification TT–W–546 and AWPA Standard P5, 31.8 percent copper oxide and 68.2 percent chromic acid. Equivalent amounts of copper sulfate, potassium dichromate, or sodium dichromate may be used in place of copper oxide. Tests on stakes and posts exposed to decay and termite attack indicate that wood well impregnated with Celcure gives good service. Tests by the Forest Products Laboratory and the U.S. Navy showed that wood thoroughly impregnated with at least 0.5 p.c.f. of Celcure has some resistance to marine borer attack. The protection against marine borers, however, is much less than that provided by a standard treatment with creosote.

Ammoniacal Copper Arsenite

According to Federal Specification TT–W–549 and AWPA Standard P5, ammoniacal copper arsenite (Chemonite) should contain approximately 49.8 percent copper oxide or an equivalent amount of copper hydroxide, 50.2 percent of arsenic pentoxide or an equivalent amount of arsenic trioxide, and 1.7 percent of acetic acid. The net retention of preservative is calculated as pounds of copper oxide plus arsenic pentoxide per cubic foot of wood treated within the proportions in the specification.

Service records on structures treated with ammoniacal copper arsenite show that this preservative provides very good protection against decay and termites. High retentions of preservative will provide extended service life to wood exposed to the marine environment, provided pholad-type borers are not present.

Chromated Copper Arsenate

Types I, II, and III of chromated copper arsentate are covered in Federal Specification TT–W–550 and AWPA Standard P5. The compositions of the three types according to that Federal specification are:

	Type I	Type II	Type III
		Parts by weight	
Chromium trioxide	61	35.3	47
Copper oxide	17	19.6	19
Arsenic pentoxide	22	45.1	34

The above types permit substitution of potassium or sodium dichromate for chromium trioxide; copper sulfate, basic copper carbonate, or copper hydroxide for copper oxide; and arsenic acid or sodium arsenate for arsenic pentoxide.

Type I (Erdalith, Greensalt, Tanalith, CCA)

Service data on treated poles, posts, and stakes installed in the United States since 1938 have shown excellent protection against decay fungi and termites. High retentions of copper chrome arsenate-treated wood have shown good resistance to marine borer attack when only Limnoria and teredo borers are present.

Type II (Boliden K–33)

This preservative has been used commercially in Sweden since 1950 and now throughout the world. It was included in stake tests in the United States in 1949 and commercial use in the United States started in 1964.

Type III (Wolman CCA)

Composition of this preservative was arrived at by AWPA technical committees in encouraging a single standard for chromated copper arsenate preservatives. Commercial preservatives of similar composition have been tested and used in England since 1954 and more recently in Australia, New Zealand, Malaysia, and in various countries of Africa and Central Europe and are performing very well.

Chromated Zinc Chloride

Chromated zinc chloride is covered in Federal Specification TT–W–551 and in AWPA Standard P5. Chromated zinc chloride (FR)[1]

---

[1] Designation for fire retardant.

is included, as a fire-retarding chemical, in AWPA Standard P10.

Chromated zinc chloride was developed about 1934. The specifications require that it contain 80 percent of zinc oxide and 20 percent of chromium trioxide. Zinc chloride may be substituted for the zinc oxide and sodium dichromate for the chromium trioxide. The preservative is only moderately effective in contact with the ground or in wet installations but has performed well under somewhat drier conditions. Its principal advantages are its low cost and ease of handling at treating plants.

Chromated zinc chloride (FR) contains 80 percent of chromated zinc chloride, 10 percent of boric acid, and 10 percent of ammonium sulfate. Retentions of from $1\frac{1}{2}$ to 3 p.c.f. of wood provide combined protection from fire, decay, and insect attack.

Fluor Chrome Arsenate Phenol

The composition of fluor chrome arsenate phenol (FCAP) is included in Federal Specification TT–W–535 and the AWPA Standard P5. The active ingredients of this preservative are:

	Percent
Fluoride	22
Chromium trioxide	37
Arsenic pentoxide	25
Dinitrophenol	16

To avoid objectionable staining of building materials, sodium pentachlorophenate is sometimes substituted in equal amounts for the dinitrophenol.

Sodium or potassium fluoride may be used as a source of fluoride. Sodium chromate or dichromate may be used in place of chromium trioxide. Sodium arsenate may be used in place of arsenic pentoxide.

FCAP type I (Wolman salts) and FCAP type II (Osmosalts) have performed well in above-ground wood structures and given moderate protection when used in contact with the ground.

PRESERVATIVE EFFECTIVENESS

Preservative effectiveness is influenced not only by the protective value of the preservative chemical itself, but also by the method of application and extent of penetration and retention of the preservative in the treated wood. Even with an effective preservative, good protection cannot be expected with poor penetration and substandard retentions. The species of wood, proportion of heartwood and sapwood, heartwood penetrability, and moisture content are among the important variables influencing the results of treatment.

Results of service tests on various treated products that show the effectiveness of different wood preservatives are published periodically in the proceedings of the American Wood-Preservers' Association and elsewhere. Few service tests, however, include a variety of preservatives under comparable conditions of exposure. Furthermore, service tests may not show a good comparison between different preservatives due to the difficulty in controlling the above-mentioned variables.

APPLYING PRESERVATIVES

Wood-preserving methods are of two general types: (1) Pressure processes, in which the wood is impregnated in closed vessels under pressures considerably above atmospheric, and (2) nonpressure processes, which vary widely as to procedures and equipment used. Pressure processes generally provide a closer control over preservative retentions and penetrations, and usually provide greater protection than nonpressure processes. Some nonpressure methods, however, are better than others and are occasionally as effective as pressure processes in providing good preservative retentions and penetrations.

Pressure Processes

In commercial practice, wood is most often treated by immersing it in preservative in high-pressure apparatus and applying pressure to drive the preservative into the wood. Pressure processes differ in details, but the general principle is the same. The wood, on cars, is run into a long steel cylinder (fig. 18–3), which is then closed and filled with preservative. Pressure forces preservative into the wood until the desired amount has been absorbed. Considerable preservative is absorbed, with relatively deep penetration. Two processes, the full-cell and empty-cell, are in common use.

Nonpressure Processes

The numerous nonpressure processes differ widely in the penetrations and retentions of preservative attained and consequently in the degree of protection they provide to the treated wood. When similar retentions and penetrations are achieved, wood treated by a nonpressure method should have a service life comparable to that of wood treated by pressure. Nevertheless, results of nonpressure treatments, particularly those involving superficial applications, are not generally as satisfactory as pressure treatment. The superficial processes do serve a useful purpose when more thorough treatments are either impractical or exposure conditions are such that little preservative protection is required.

Nonpressure methods, in general, consist of: (1) Superficial applications of preservative oils by spraying, brushing, or brief dipping; (2) soaking in preservative oils or steeping in solutions of waterborne preservatives; (3) diffusion processes with waterborne preservatives; (4) various adaptations of the thermal or hot-and-cold bath process; (5) vacuum treatment; and (6) a variety of miscellaneous processes.

Superficial Applications

The simplest treatment is to apply the preservative—creosote or other oils—to the wood with a brush or a spray nozzle. Oils that are throughly liquid when cold should be selected, unless it is possible to heat the preservative. The oil should be flooded over the wood, rather than merely painted upon it. Every check and depression in the wood should be thoroughly filled with the preservative, because any untreated wood left exposed provides ready access for fungi. Rough lumber may require as much as 10 gallons of oil per 1,000 square feet of surface, but surfaced lumber requires considerably less. The transverse penetrations obtained will usually be less than $1/10$ inch although, in easily penetrated species, end grain (longitudinal) penetration is considerably greater.

Brush and spray treatments should be used only when more effective treatments cannot be employed. The additional life obtained by such treatments over that of untreated wood will be affected greatly by the conditions of service; for wood in contact with the ground, it may be from 1 to 5 years.

Dipping for a few seconds to several minutes in a preservative oil gives greater assurance (than brushing or spraying) that all surfaces and checks are thoroughly coated with the oil; usually it results in slightly greater penetrations. It is a common practice to treat window sash, frames, and other millwork, either before or after assembly, by dipping for approximately 3 minutes in a water-repellent preservative. Such treatment is covered by Commercial Standard CS–262, which also provides for equivalent treatment by the vacuum process. The amount of preservative used may vary from about 6 to 17 gallons per thousand board feet (0.5 to 1.5 p.c.f.) of millwork treated.

The penetration of preservative into end surfaces of ponderosa pine sapwood is, in some cases, as much as 1 to 3 inches. End penetration in such woods as southern pine and Douglas-fir, however, is much less, particularly in the heartwood. Transverse penetration of the preservative applied by brief dipping is very shallow, usually only a few hundredths of an inch. Since the exposed end surfaces at joints are the most vulnerable to decay in millwork products, good end penetration is especially advantageous. Dip applications provide very limited protection to wood used in contact with the ground or under very moist conditions, and they provide very limited protection against attack by termites. They do have value, however, for exterior woodwork. and millwork that is painted, that is not in contact with the ground, and that is exposed to moisture only for brief periods at a time.

Cold Soaking and Steeping

Cold soaking well-seasoned wood for several hours or days in low-viscosity preservative oils or steeping green or seasoned wood for several days in waterborne preservatives have provided varying success on fenceposts, lumber, and timbers.

Pine posts treated by cold soaking for 24 to 48 hours or longer, in a solution containing 5 percent of pentachlorophenol in No. 2 fuel oil, have shown an average life of 16 to 20 years or longer. The sapwood in these posts was well penetrated and preservative solution retentions ranged from 2 to 6 p.c.f. Most species do not treat as satisfactorily as the pines by cold soaking, and test posts of such woods as birch, aspen, and sweetgum treated by this method have failed in much shorter times.

Preservative penetrations and retentions obtained by cold soaking lumber for several hours are considerably better than those obtained by brief dipping of similar species. Preservative retentions, however, seldom equal those obtained in pressure treatment except in cases such as sapwood of pines that has become highly absorptive through mold and stain infection.

Steeping with waterborne preservatives has very limited use in the United States but has been employed for many years in Europe. In treating seasoned wood both the water and the preservative salt in the solution soak into the wood. With green wood, the preservative enters the water-saturated wood by diffusion. Preservative retentions and penetrations vary over a wide range, and the process is not generally recommended when more reliable treatments are practical.

Diffusion Processes

In addition to the steeping process, diffusion processes are used with green or wet wood. These processes employ waterborne preservatives that will diffuse out of the water of the treating solution or paste into the water of the wood.

The double-diffusion process developed by the Forest Products Laboratory has shown very good results in post tests, particularly on full-length immersion treatments. It consists of steeping green or partially seasoned wood first in one chemical and then in another. The two chemicals diffuse into the wood and then react to precipitate an effective preservative with high resistance to leaching. The process has had commercial application in cooling towers where preservative protection is needed to avoid early replacement.

Other diffusion processes involve applying preservatives to the butts or around the groundline of posts or poles. In standing-pole treatments the preservative may be injected into the pole at groundline with a special tool, applied on the pole surface as a paste or bandage, poured into holes bored in the pole at the groundline, or poured on the surface of the pole and into an excavation several inches deep around the groundline of the pole. These treatments have recognized value for application to untreated standing poles and to treated poles where preservative retentions are determined to be inadequate.

Effect of Treatment on Strength

Coal-tar creosote, creosote-coal-tar mixtures, creosote-petroleum oil mixtures, and pentachlorophenol dissolved in petroleum oils are practically inert to wood and have no chemical influence that would affect its strength. Likewise, solutions containing standard waterborne preservatives, in the concentrations commonly used in preservative treatment, have limited or no important effect on the strength of wood.

Although wood preservatives are not harmful in themselves, injecting them into the wood may result in considerable loss in wood strength if the treatment is unusually severe or not properly carried out. Factors that influence the effect of the treating process on strength include (1) species of wood, (2) size and moisture content of the timbers treated, (3) heating medium used and its temperature, (4) length of the heating period in conditioning the wood for treatment and time the wood is in the hot preservative, and (5) amount of pressure used. Most important of these factors are the severity and duration of the heating conditions used.

HANDLING AND SEASONING TIMBER AFTER TREATMENT

Treated timber should be handled with sufficient care to avoid breaking through the treated areas. The use of pikes, cant hooks, picks, tongs, or other pointed tools that dig deeply into the wood should be prohibited. Handling heavy loads of lumber or sawed timber in rope or cable slings may crush the corners or edges of the outside pieces. Breakage or deep abrasions may also result from throwing the lumber or dropping it. If damage results, the exposed places should be re-treated as thoroughly as conditions permit. Long storage of treated wood before installation should be avoided because such storage encourages deep and detrimental checking and may also result in significant loss of some preservatives. Treated wood that must be stored before use should be covered for protection from the sun and weather.

Although cutting wood after treatment is highly undesirable, it cannot always be avoided. When cutting is necessary, the damage may be partly overcome in timber for land or fresh-water use by a thorough application of a grease containing 10 percent pentachlorophenol. This provides a protective reservoir of preservative on the surface, some of which may slowly migrate into the end grain of the wood. Thoroughly brushing the cut surfaces with two coats of hot creosote is also helpful, although brush coating cut surfaces gives little protection against marine borers. A special device is available for pressure treating bolt holes bored after treatment. For wood treated with waterborne preservatives, where the use of creosote or pentachlorophenol solution on the cut surfaces is not practicable, a 5 percent solution of the waterborne preservative in use should be substituted.

For treating the end surfaces of piles where they are cut off after driving, at least two generous coats of creosote should be applied. A coat of asphalt or similar material may well applied over the creosote, followed by some protective sheet material, such as metal, roofing felt, or saturated fabric, fitted over the pile head and brought down the sides far enough to protect against damage to the top treatment and against the entrance of storm water. AWPA standard M4 contains instructions for the care of pressure-treated wood after treatment.

Wood treated with preservative oils should generally be installed as soon as practicable after treatment but some times cleanliness of the surface can be improved by exposure to the weather for a limited time before use. Waterborne preservatives or pentachlorophenol in a volatile solvent, however, are best suited to uses where cleanliness or paintability are of great importance.

With waterborne preservatives, seasoning after treatment is important for wood to be used in buildings or other places where shrinkage after placement in the structure would be undesirable. Injecting waterborne preservatives puts large amounts of water into the wood, and considerable shrinkage is to be expected as subsequent seasoning takes place. For best results, the wood should be dried to approximately the moisture content it will ultimately reach in service. During drying, the wood should be carefully piled, and whenever possible, restrained by sufficient weight on the top of the pile to avoid warping.

With some waterborne preservatives, seasoning after treatment is recommended for all treated wood. During this seasoning period, volatile chemicals escape and the chemical reactions are completed within the wood; thus, the resistance of the preservative to leaching by water is increased.

References

(1) American Institute of Timber Construction. 1966. Timber construction manual. Englewood, Colo. 80110.

(2) American Wood-Preservers' Association. AWPA standards. (Revised as needed.) Washington, D. C. 20005.

(3) Anderson, L. O. 1967. Selection and use of wood products for home and farm building. Agriculture Information Bulletin No. 311. U. S. Government Printing Office, Washington, D. C. 20402.

(4) California Redwood Association. 1971. Redwood decks. San Francisco, Calif. 94111.

(5) Lane Book Co. 1963. How to build decks for outdoor living. Menlo Park, Calif. 94025.

(6) Southern Forest Products Association. n.d. Decks .... Patios .... Fences. Technical Bulletin No. 14. Metairie, La. 70002.

(7) U. S. Department of Agriculture. 1970. Forest Products Laboratory natural finish. Research Note FPL-046. Forest Products Laboratory, Forest Service, Madison, Wis. 53705.

(8) _____ 1966. Wood finishing: painting outside wood surfaces. Research Note FPL-0123. Forest Products Laboratory, Forest Service, Madison, Wis. 53705.

(9) _____ 1955. Wood handbook. Agriculture Handbook No. 72. U. S. Government Printing Office, Washington, D. C. 20402.

(10) U. S. Department of Commerce. 1966. U. S. Product Standard PS 1-66 for softwood plywood. National Bureau of Standards, Washington, D. C. 20230. Also available from American Plywood Association, Tacoma, Wash. 98401.

(11) U. S. Department of Housing & Urban Development. 1967. FHA pole house construction. Washington, D. C. 20402.

(12) Verrall, Arthur F. 1966. Building decay associated with rain seepage. U. S. Department of Agriculture, Forest Service, Technical Bulletin 1356, U. S. Government Printing Office, Washington, D. C. 20402.

(13) Western Wood Products Association. n.d. Western wood decks. Portland, Oregon 97204.

Glossary

acrylic resin — a thermoplastic resin used in latex coatings (see latex paint).

air-dried — dried by exposure to air, usually in a yard, without artificial heat.

alkyd resin — one of a large group of synthetic resins used in making latex paints.

baluster — small vertical member in a railing, between a top rail and a stair tread or bottom rail.

bending strength — the resistance of a member when loaded like a beam.

butt joint — the junction where the ends of two members meet in a square-cut joint.

cant strip — a piece of lumber triangular in cross section, used at the junction of a flat deck and a wall to avoid a sharp bend and possible cracking of the covering which is applied over it.

caulk — to make a seam watertight by filling it with a waterproofing compound.

countersink — to set the head of a nail or screw at or below the surface.

creosote — a distillate of coal tar produced by high temperature carbonization of bituminous coal; it consists principally of liquid and solid aromatic hydrocarbons; used as a wood preservative.

dado cuts — rectangular grooves in a board or plank.

dead load — load imposed by the weight of the materials that make up the structure.

decay — the decomposition of wood or other substance by fungi.

elastomeric — having elastic, rubber-like properties.

flashing — sheet metal or other material used in construction to protect from water seepage.

grouted — filled with a mortar thin enough to fill the spaces in the concrete or ground around the object being set.

gusset plate — a flat wood, plywood, or similar type member used to provide a connection at intersection of wood members.

header — a beam placed perpendicular to joists and to which joists are nailed in framing.

heartwood — older wood from the central portion of the tree. As this wood ceases to participate in the life process of the tree, it undergoes chemical changes that often impart a resistance to decay and a darkening in color.

kiln-dried — dried in a kiln with the use of artificial heat.

lag screws — large screws with heads designed to be turned with a wrench.

latex paint — a coating in which the vehicle is a water emulsion of rubber or synthetic resin.

ledger — a strip of lumber nailed along the side of a girder or wall, on which joists rest.

liquified gas — a carrier of wood preservatives, this is a hydrocarbon that is a gas at atmospheric pressure but one that can be liquified at moderate pressures (similar to propane).

live load — load superimposed on the structure by occupancy, furniture, snow, etc.

moisture content — the amount of water contained in wood, expressed as a percentage of the weight of the oven-dry wood.

neoprene — a synthetic rubber characterized by superior resistance to oils, gasoline, and sunlight.

non-leachable — not dissolved and removed by the action of rain or other water.

pentachlorophenol (penta) — a chlorinated phenol, usually in petroleum oil, used as a wood preservative.

penta grease — a penta-petroleum emulsion system suspended in water by the use of emulsifiers and dispersing agents.

Plugged Exterior — a grade of plywood used

for subfloor underlayment. The knot holes in the face plys are plugged and the surface is touch-sanded.

primer or prime coat — the first coat in a paint job that consists of two or more coats. The primer may have special properties that provide an improved base for the finish coat.

racking resistance — a resistance to forces in the plane of a structure that tend to force it out of shape.

silicone — one of a large group of polymerized organic siloxanes that are available as resins, coatings, sealants, etc., with excellent waterproofing characteristics.

stiffness — resistance to deformation by loads that cause bending stresses.

superstructure — the structural part of the deck above the posts or supports.

T&G — tongue and grooved joining of ends or edges.

Underlayment Exterior — see Plugged Exterior.

water-repellent preservative — a liquid designed to penetrate into wood and impart water repellency and a moderate preservative protection. It is usually applied by dipping.